The Norton Manual of Music Notation

The
NORTON
MANUAL
of
MUSIC
NOTATION

by

George Heussenstamm

W. W. Norton & Company · New York · London

Copyright © 1987 by W. W. Norton & Company, Inc.
All rights reserved.
Printed in the United States of America.

The text of this book is composed in Caslon.
Composition and manufacturing by The Maple-Vail Book Group.

First Edition

Library of Congress Cataloging-in-Publication Data

Heussenstamm, George.
  The Norton manual of music notation.
  Bibliography: p.
  1. Musical notation. I. Title.
MT35.H55 1987   781′.24   86-16449

ISBN 0-393-95526-5

W. W. Norton & Company, Inc., 500 Fifth Avenue, New York, N.Y. 10110
W. W. Norton & Company Ltd., 10 Coptic Street, London WC1A 1PU

4 5 6 7 8 9 0

Contents

PREFACE

When you, the music student, enter college, it is reasonable to assume that you have some background in performance and a nodding acquaintance with the rudiments of music. Although you have probably seen a great deal of music in your precollege experience and have learned to read and play its rhythms and pitches, a problem may arise the moment you enter your first theory class and try to write notes on paper. The principles of notation, although implicit in the printed music with which you are familiar, have rarely been isolated, examined, and codified. As a result, your written assignments may be bristling with errors and your ability to communicate your intentions seriously impaired.

This manual was designed to alleviate that problem in several ways: (1) by presenting the principles of music notation as clearly and simply as possible; (2) by showing you how to produce music manuscript which is not only correct in terms of notation, but legibly and swiftly written; and (3) by introducing the full range of writing tools from the simple pencil to the music copyist's pen.

For the music student and the advanced composer and arranger alike, this manual provides answers to vital questions concerning music notation and manuscript preparation. The elements of notation are described in order of complexity; pencil (or felt-tip pen) is the basic writing instrument. The various appendices are devoted to the materials and techniques employed in copying music with pen and ink, and cover the procedures which will ultimately produce the finished score.

Parts I and II deal with music written on a single staff—first as a single line of notes, then as two lines of notes. In Part III, music on two or more staves, from simple piano notation to full orchestral score, is discussed. The manual is organized for maximum accessibility and clarity; it is not meant to be studied *ad seriatim*, but should be used according to your needs.

One final caveat: since this is a manual devoted to basic procedures in music notation, brevity and concision have been our constant watchwords. You will not find special instrumental signs or theory symbols herein, and are therefore urged to refer, when appropriate, to a good orchestration text, a theory book, etc.

PART ONE

Elements of Notation

BASIC WRITING
MATERIALS

The only writing instrument required in this manual is a pencil or a felt-tip pen. I recommend that you use a high quality #2 pencil (Venus, Eagle, Dixon, etc.) or a .7 or .9 millimeter automatic pencil with a medium–soft lead. A separate, white plastic eraser is helpful. If you use a felt-tip pen, experiment with several before deciding which brand is most comfortable for you to work with.

Ideally, hand-written music should resemble printed music as much as possible. For this reason, the examples in this book were drawn with a music-copying pen with which one can simulate the varying thickness of the vertical and horizontal lines in engraved music. When you work with a pencil, however, it is too time consuming to trouble with these differences in thickness. Written music with all of the visual refinements of engraved music is better produced with the music pen, which is dealt with in the Appendix. Therefore, your work should look more like Example 1–1a than 1–1b.

Example 1–1

a. Pencil

b. Music Pen

Straight vertical and horizontal lines contribute greatly to the legibility of a hand-written manuscript. For this purpose, a clear plastic right triangle is extremely useful. It comes in various sizes, the most convenient being 3½″ by 6″. Keep the short side in the vertical plane and use it to draw all barlines, stems, and the vertical lines of all accidentals. The long side is used to draw beams, wedges, and any other more or less horizontal lines.

Example 1–2   The 30°–60° Right Triangle

Draw horizontal lines from left to right along the top edge of the triangle.

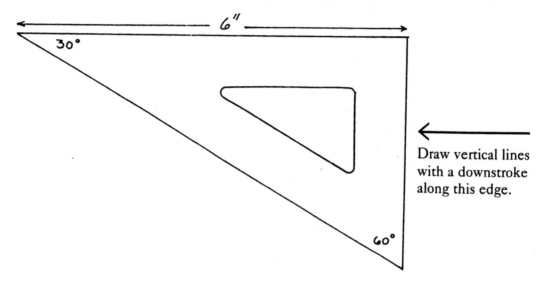

Draw vertical lines
with a downstroke
along this edge.

The results you obtain with the right triangle are vastly superior to freehand writing and the process is easy to master. (See the Appendix for the right triangle used with pen and ink.)

For the most part, written assignments in theory classes do not require special manuscript paper. The college bookstore will have 8½″ × 11″ music paper which will serve your purposes for the time being quite adequately. For more complex projects in orchestration or composition courses, special papers will be needed (see pages 144–45).

Before we examine the individual elements of music notation in detail, let us see how these elements fit together in a short music example. The symbols are listed in the order in which they appear in the text.

Example 1–3

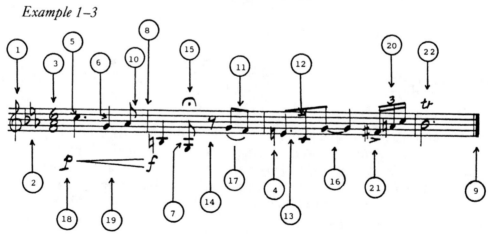

1. Clef (treble clef)
2. Key Signature
3. Time Signature (meter)
4. Accidental (natural)
5. Notehead (dotted quarter note)
6. Stem
7. Ledger lines
8. Barline
9. Terminal Barline
10. Flag
11. Beam
12. Short Beam
13. Augmentation Dot
14. Rest (eighth rest)
15. Pause (fermata)
16. Tie
17. Slur
18. Dynamic *(piano)*
19. Dynamic (crescendo wedge)
20. Irregular Subdivision of the Beat (triplet)
21. Articulation (accent)
22. Ornamentation (trill)

CLEFS

There are four clefs in common use today: treble clef, bass clef, and the two surviving members of the C-clef family, the alto and tenor clefs. The traditional treble clef is one continuous curved line, with the upper part of the curve extending about one space above the staff, and the bottom curve extending the same distance below the staff. A simpler, stylized treble clef is wholly acceptable and easier to draw.

Example 1–4

Traditional

Stylized

If you prefer the look of the traditional clef, practice drawing it beginning your continuous curve either at the bottom or in the middle. Try to be consistent.

Example 1–5

Start from bottom   Start from middle

  or

If you prefer the stylized version, draw a descending vertical line, then add the curved line starting from the top.

Example 1–6

The continuous curve of the bass clef centers around the fourth line of the staff, ending just below the second line. Use a clockwise motion in the stroke.

Example 1–7

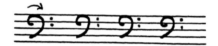

As with the treble clef, a stylized form of alto and tenor clef may be used instead of the traditional form. Use a downstroke for both vertical lines of the C clefs.

Example 1–8

| Traditional
Alto Clef | Stylized
Alto Clef | Traditional
Tenor Clef | Stylized
Tenor Clef |

DRILL

Practice writing the four clefs on the staff lines provided below. Experiment with both traditional and stylized forms.

KEY SIGNATURES

Key signatures always follow clef signs. Note that the layout of flats follows the same downward pattern in *all* clefs, whereas the pattern for sharps takes on a new contour in the tenor clef.*

Example 1–9

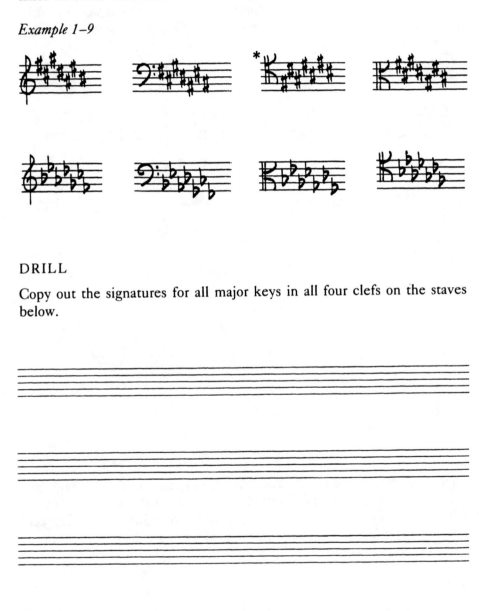

DRILL

Copy out the signatures for all major keys in all four clefs on the staves below.

TIME SIGNATURES

The time signature is placed immediately after the key signature at the beginning of a piece. Once the time signature has been established, it is not necessary to repeat it *unless* there is a change of meter. Key signatures must be carried from line to line throughout a work; this is not true for time signatures. Traditionally, the time signature is written within the confines of the staff.

Example 1–10

Common Time   Alla Breve

There is currently a growing tendency to enlarge the numbers so that they extend above and below the staff lines, giving them greater legibility. If you choose this approach, use it consistently.

Example 1–11

ACCIDENTALS

Perhaps the most carelessly written symbols in music are the accidentals. Their proportions are rather subtle and require some attention to be drawn perfectly. Use a downstroke for drawing the vertical lines. For flats the vertical line is slightly over two staff spaces long. Draw the curved portion with a clockwise motion.

Example 1–12

For naturals, use the same vertical line length, about two staff spaces. Notice the slight upward angle of the horizontal lines, about 25 degrees.

Example 1–13

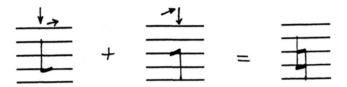

The vertical lines for sharps are almost three staff spaces long and are aligned at approximately the same upward angle that you have seen in the natural sign above. The horizontal lines also follow the same angle.

Example 1–14

Be sure to allow enough space to show through the enclosed area of all three signs. The example below shows correct and incorrect versions of these important symbols.

Example 1–15

Correct   Incorrect

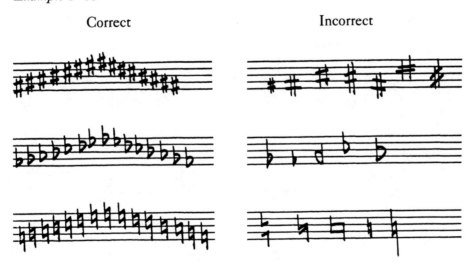

The double sharp may be written quite simply and will be quite as comprehensible as the somewhat complicated traditional form used in engraved music. A cross is all that is necessary.

Example 1–16

The double flat offers no new challenges. It is drawn in either of two ways: (1) the flats just touching each other; (2) the flats close together but not touching.

Example 1–17

Once you understand how to write the various accidentals, strive for consistency of size and shape. You should spend a considerable amount of time perfecting these elusive signs. Rest assured, you will have ample opportunity to use them.

DRILL

Copy the sequence of accidentals below on the blank staves provided for that purpose.

NOTEHEADS AND STEMS

All noteheads, with the exception of the whole note, have an *oval* shape tilted to the right:

Example 1–18

Ideally, the whole note does not tilt and is slightly larger than the half note.

Example 1–19

In common copying practice, however, whole notes are often written with the same notehead as the half note (compare the traditional form with the optional form).

Example 1–20

Traditional   Optional

In this handbook, we will use the optional form, since it is easier to draw and serves most purposes quite adequately.

HOW TO DRAW A NOTEHEAD

Half note: Beginning at the lowest left-hand corner, use a smooth clockwise motion:

Example 1–21

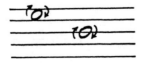

Quarter note: Begin your stroke between the staff lines with a clockwise spiral motion, gradually filling out the space until the notehead just touches the lines above and below.

Example 1–22

Use the same method, maintaining the same size and shape, when drawing a notehead on a line:

Example 1–23

An alternative technique is to draw the notehead for a half note, then fill in the space. Remember, however, that the quarter notehead is slightly smaller than the half notehead.

DRILL

Copy the notes in the example below on the blank staves provided. Try to duplicate the exact tilt and basic shape of the original noteheads.

Stems should be *one octave in length*. (Exceptions to this rule will be dealt with as they come up.)

Notes *below* the center line of the staff require an *up*-stem:

Example 1–24

Notes *above* the center line receive a *down*-stem:

Example 1–25

Notes *on* the center line may have up-stems or down-stems, depending on the notes immediately around them. However, if musical context is not a factor, write the stem *down*.

Example 1–26

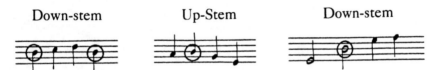

Whether the stem goes up or down from the notehead, it should always be drawn with a downstroke.

Example 1–27

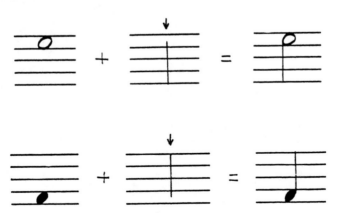

DRILL

Copy the notes of the example below on the blank lines provided. Position the accidentals so that each clearly relates to the note following it. As a further practice in drawing stems, go back to the Drill on page 10 and add stems where appropriate, noting the rule for stem direction.

LEDGER LINES

Ledger (also spelled *leger*) lines are the upward and downward extensions of staff lines and are spaced identically. They may be drawn as thin as staff lines (the traditional approach) or may be represented by a thicker line (the optional technique, usually produced by a music pen). All of the examples in this handbook employ the optional alternative, since it saves time.

Example 1–28

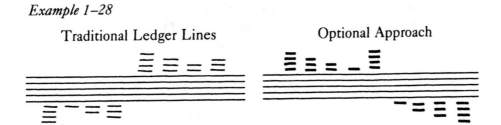

Ledger lines should be twice the width of a notehead. They should extend clearly beyond each side of the notehead.

Example 1–29

We now encounter the first modification of the rule for stem length: when writing notes two or more ledger lines above or below the staff, the stems are lengthened to reach the center line of the staff.

Example 1–30

These stems are too short.

OCTAVE SIGNS

Octave signs are used to avoid excessive and confusing ledger lines. "8va" or "8," written *above* the staff, indicates that the passage is to be performed one octave higher than written. "15ma" or "15" indicates that the music should be played *two* octaves higher.* If these signs are placed *below* the staff, the notes are sounded one or two octaves lower than written. The word "bassa" (below) is sometimes added to the latter.

Each sign is followed by a dotted line ending with a short vertical stroke. Here the word "loco" (place) is often added to emphasize that the music is once again to be played at its normal pitch.

Example 1–31

a.

b.

c.

---

* "va" is an abbreviation of the Italian word for octave, *ottava;* the "ma" in "15ma" refers to the Italian word for a fifteenth (two octaves), *quindicesima.* Avoid the incorrect "15va."

DRILL

Copy the notes of the examples below on the blank staves provided. As you work, bear in mind the shape and size of noteheads; stem lengths; shape, size, and placement of accidentals; and the width and alignment of ledger lines.

BARLINES

A barline is a vertical line drawn through the staff to mark off measures. Always use a downstroke to write a barline. Practice drawing barlines by writing several, trying to space them as evenly as possible. Use the triangle to help you or, if you can trust it, your well-controlled freehand. The result should be a consistently straight vertical line.

Example 1–32   Single Barline

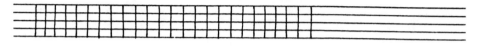

(For your practice)

Use an interior double bar for the ends of sections and before any change of key. It consists of two simple barlines close to one another.

Example 1–33   Interior Double Barline

(For your practice)

The terminal double bar is made by drawing three barlines close together and filling in the space between the second and third lines.

Example 1–34   Terminal Double Barline

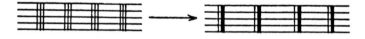

(For your practice)

INTERVALS AND CHORDS

INTERVALS

Two notes sounded simultaneously are often written on a single stem and thus consideration must be given to: (1) stem direction; (2) stem length; and (3) note placement on stem.

Stem direction is determined by the note that is farthest away from the center line of the staff:

Example 1–35

This note is farthest from the center line;
therefore the stem goes *down*.

This note is farthest from the center line;
therefore, the stem goes *up*.

If the two notes are equidistant from the center line, the stem may go either up or down.

Example 1–36

Musical context may play a determining role.

Example 1–37

Stem down

Stem up

Stem length is normally 2½ to 3 staff spaces beyond the note nearest the stem ending.

Example 1–38

When ledger lines have to be used for intervals on one stem, be sure that the stem is extended at least to the center line.

Example 1–39

Larger intervals involving ledger lines may call for stem lengths that go beyond the center line.

Example 1–40

Note placement on stem: When two notes on one stem form the interval of a second, the *lower* of the two notes is positioned on the *left* side of the stem.

Example 1–41

When the interval of a second is presented on ledger lines, the ledger line must be widened to accommodate both notes and retain a bit of line on each side of each note:

Example 1–42

Ledger lines extended →

← Ledger lines extended

CHORDS

When chords contain three or more notes, the same rules apply: stem direction is determined by the note *farthest from the center line.*

Example 1–43

If all the notes are equidistant from the center, the stem can go up or down.

Example 1–44

However, if the outer notes are equidistant from the center, an inner note may be the determining factor in stem direction. Both examples below are acceptable, but the one on the left is preferable because it appears to be better balanced.

Example 1–45

Preferable   Acceptable

In any chord containing the interval of a second, the lower note of the two
is placed to the left of the stem, as in Example 1–41.

Example 1–46

Remember that the only notes ever placed on the "wrong" side of the stem
are notes that are part of the interval of a second. Compare the correct and
incorrect placement of the notes in the chords below:

Example 1–47

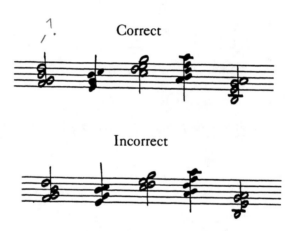

Chords written in whole notes are arranged *as if* they had stems. Compare
the correct and incorrect versions below:

Example 1–48

ACCIDENTALS IN INTERVALS AND CHORDS

Very clear guidelines exist for the placement of accidentals in intervals and chords.

1. If an interval or chord contains *two* accidentals, and they are a seventh or more apart, the accidentals are placed in normal position next to the notehead.

Example 1–49

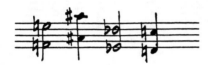

2. If the noteheads are less than a seventh apart, the lower of the two accidentals must be placed to the *left* of the upper accidental so the two do not touch.

Example 1–50

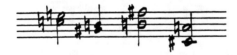

Always write accidentals in normal size; don't make them smaller in order to keep them close to the noteheads.

Example 1–51

A good basic rule to remember is: *Start at the top and work your way down.* When you have three accidentals in a chord, place the top one next to its note. Then position the middle accidental far enough to the left to leave enough room for the lowest accidental to clear both upper accidentals.

Example 1–52

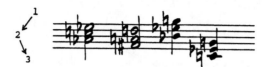

If there is a distance of a seventh or more between any of the two notes, only one accidental will have to be placed to the left.

Example 1–53

The following are the patterns for placement of *four*, *five*, and *six* accidentals:

Example 1–54

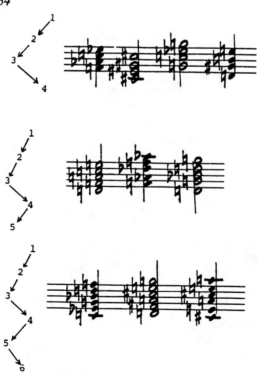

Similarly, if sufficient distance exists between noteheads, these patterns may be changed.

Example 1–55

Chords containing seconds may or may not conform to the general rules. Observe how the particular configuration of each chord calls for individual decisions in accidental placement.

Example 1–56

Most of the time, the basic rule applies quite satisfactorily. With a little practice, you should be able to determine with ease the proper placement of accidentals in chords containing one or more seconds, or chords with wide enough spacing of noteheads to require a modification of the standard pattern for accidentals.

FLAGS AND BEAMS

FLAGS

The flag (tail, pennant) is a curved shape which, when attached to the stems of single notes, converts quarter notes into eighth, sixteenth, thirty-second, or sixty-fourth notes. Notice that the flag forms a point at the stem end, that it curves a bit like the letter "s," and that its termination points in the direction of the notehead.

Example 1–57   Drawing the Eighth Note

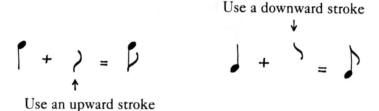

DRILL

Copy the notes in the example below on the blank lines provided, striving for uniformity and consistency.

The sixteenth-note stem is the same length as that of the eighth note (one octave). Its outer flag (farthest from the notehead) is shortened and the inner flag closely resembles the eighth-note flag, although it is slightly smaller. The distance between the two flags is a bit less than one staff space.

Example 1–58 Drawing the Sixteenth Note

For the thirty-second and sixty-fourth notes, the stem must be lengthened to accommodate the additional flags. The outer flags are short and the inner flag is more curved. The space between flags must be even and the shape of all outer flags should be uniform.

Example 1–59 Drawing the Thirty-Second Note

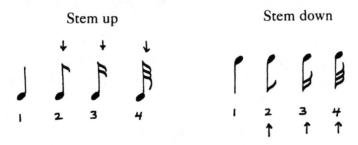

Example 1–60 Drawing the Sixty-Fourth Note

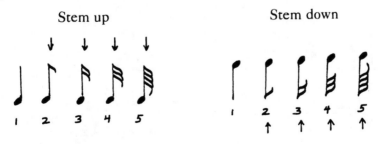

When flagged notes are to be written on ledger lines, two rules must be carefully observed: (1) a flag should never touch a ledger line; (2) the stem must be extended to the center line for an eighth note, and still further for the other flagged notes.

Example 1–61   Some Examples of Flagged Notes on Ledger Lines

BEAMS

A beam is a thick horizontal line used in place of flags where a group of two or more notes form a metrical unit. Beamed groups are easier to read than a cluster of flagged notes. (Compare the two sets of examples below.)

Example 1–62

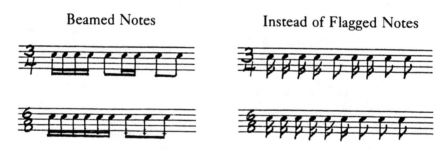

However, beams are sometimes inappropriate in certain time signatures or may have to be *combined* with flags:

Example 1–63

Avoid freehand beaming, if possible; use, instead, the long side of the right triangle. The distance between two beams of a sixteenth-note pattern is not quite as wide as a staff space. The slant of the beams depends on the contour of the group of notes. Repeated-note figures (a), patterns beginning and ending with the same note (b), and notes with a horizontally balanced contour (c) receive *horizontal* beams.

Example 1–64

When laying in beams (to connect a group of notes), adjust your stem lengths to insure that the *shortest* stem will be at least one octave long. Then adjust all other stems accordingly. Note that the stems must go through the secondary beam and reach the primary beam in all cases.

Example 1–65

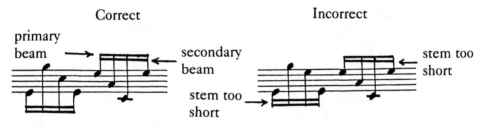

Stem direction for a group of beamed notes is determined by the note *farthest away from the middle line of the staff.* Let us examine the following groups of notes and see how we must approach the problem of drawing them correctly as sixteenth notes.

Example 1–66

In (a), the F♯ is farthest from the middle line, so the stems must go up. In (b), the G above the staff is farthest from the middle line, so the stems go down. In (c), the E♭ and F are equidistant from the center line; so are the A and C; therefore the note D determines the stem direction: down. Taking into account the total configuration of the group, we estimate the stem length of the outer notes and draw them:

Example 1–67

Then rule the beams:

Finally, draw the remaining stems.

As already mentioned, the slant of the beam is determined by the contour of the group of noteheads. It is highly advisable to follow the old engraver's rule that the tilt of a beam *should not exceed the width of one staff space*, regardless of the contour of the noteheads. The examples on the left below represent the desirable angle, whereas the examples on the right have much too sharp a beam angle.

Example 1–68

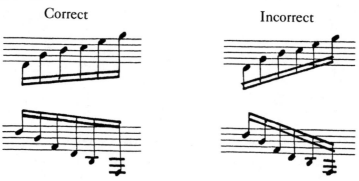

One further exception to the rules concerning the slant of beams: notes written well above or below the staff are more legible when written with horizontal beams, despite the angled contour of the pitches.

Example 1–69

Preferable   Harder to Read

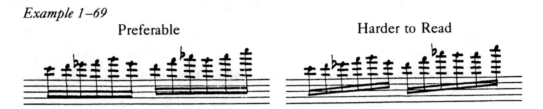

Secondary beams are frequently grouped differently from primary beams for a variety of reasons: a run of thirty-second notes is more easily read if the innermost secondary beam is broken (Example 1–70a); patterns of eighths and sixteenths are much clearer if the eighth notes are beamed with the sixteenths (Example 1–70b); a very short secondary beam makes syncopations and dotted rhythms even more explicit (Example 1–70c).

Example 1–70

(a)   (b)

(c)

DRILL

Copy the following series of notes and beam them in groups of three eighth notes, four sixteenth notes, and six thirty-second notes, as shown.

AUGMENTATION DOTS

The augmentation dot lengthens the note it modifies by half of that note's value. It is always placed to the right of the notehead. Note the slight variations in position illustrated in the example below:

Example 1–71

a. The notehead is in a space   b. The notehead is on a line

(The same rules of position apply to notes on ledger lines or between ledger lines.) In chords, *all* of the notes must be dotted, following the same basic rule.

Example 1–72

When the interval of a second is involved, it may be necessary to place a dot *below* the note it modifies (Example 1–73a, b). There may even be the odd occasion when the small cluster of tones necessitates placing a dot *on* a line (Example 1–73c).

Example 1–73

   (a)   (b)   (c)

DOUBLE DOTTING

If a single dot increases the duration of a note by one half, the double dot increases it by three fourths.

Example 1–74

(a)   (b)

(c)

DRILL

Place an augmentation dot after every notehead in the following exercise:

RESTS AND PAUSES

RESTS

Rests should be drawn to resemble those found in engraved music as closely as possible.

Quarter rests: Take the time and trouble to draw the slightly tricky quarter rest properly: in the middle of the staff and in an upright position. It has three basic components written in one continuous movement.

Example 1–75

1.   2.   3.   =   Quarter rest

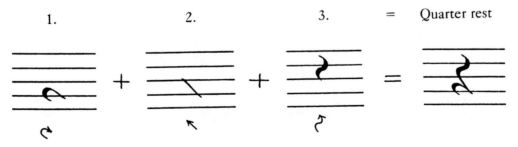

Avoid the sloppy short-cut versions such as these:

Example 1–76

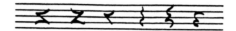

DRILL

Using Example 1–75 as a guide, draw as many quarter rests as you can fit on the following line:

Whole and half rests have the same basic shape, *but:*

> whole rests hang below the fourth line of the staff;
> half rests sit on top of the middle line;
> whole rests are always placed in the *center* of the measure.*

Example 1–77

Whole Rest　　　　　　　　Half Rests

a.　　　　　　　　b.　　　　　　　　c.

The whole rest is used in all meters except 4 / 2. For this infrequently used meter, the double whole rest is required:

Example 1–78

Shorter rests: Eighth, sixteenth, thirty-second, and sixty-fourth rests are all derived from one basic shape:

---

*except in 4/2 time where a whole rest may represent half a measure, in which case, the rest is placed in the metrically appropriate position (like the half rest in 4/4 time.

Example 1–79

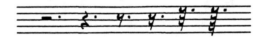

1.   2.   =   Eighth rest

The shorter the rest, the more prolongation of the vertical line is required for the additional hooks entered in the appropriate spaces between the staff lines.

Example 1–80

a. Sixteenth Rests   b. Thirty-second Rests   c. Sixty-fourth Rests

The Augmentation dot applies to rests as well as notes, especially in compound meters. Note the correct placement of the dot after various kinds of rests. Incidentally, whole rests should *never* be dotted.

Example 1–81

Current notation practice employs the dotted rest much more liberally than in the past. Compare the right- and left-hand columns of Example 1–82.

Example 1–82

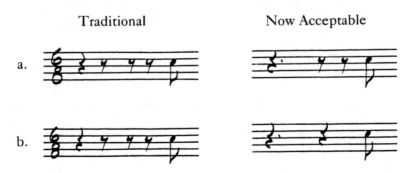

Traditional   Now Acceptable

a.

b.

Traditional   Now Acceptable

The following columns offer examples of correct and incorrect use of rests. Notice that rests are never syncopated and that meter subdivision must be clearly indicated.

Example 1–83

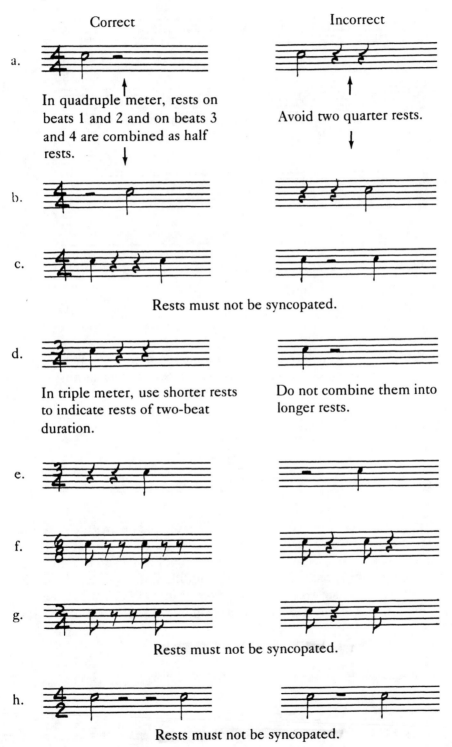

Correct   Incorrect

a.

In quadruple meter, rests on beats 1 and 2 and on beats 3 and 4 are combined as half rests.

Avoid two quarter rests.

b.

c.

Rests must not be syncopated.

d.

In triple meter, use shorter rests to indicate rests of two-beat duration.

Do not combine them into longer rests.

e.

f.

g.

Rests must not be syncopated.

h.

Rests must not be syncopated.

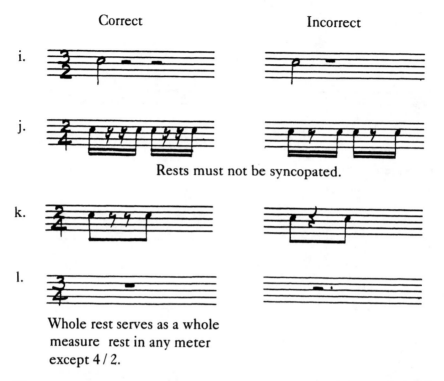

Correct   Incorrect

i.

j.

Rests must not be syncopated.

k.

l.

Whole rest serves as a whole
measure rest in any meter
except 4 / 2.

The traditional way to notate rests in combination with beamed notes is
illustrated below. Note that rests are always written in their normal position on the staff.

Example 1–84

There is a growing tendency today to employ extended beams and position
rests as if they were noteheads, often well outside their normal position
(Example 1–85a). This serves a positive purpose of clarifying the rhythm.
A refinement of this practice involves the addition of "stemlets," which
point to the exact place where the rests occur in the beat (Example 1–
85b). Both approaches are acceptable and you may use either, but be consistent.

Example 1–85

a. Extended Beams   b. Extended Beams with Stemlets

PAUSES

Fermata: There are a number of signs other than rests that indicate pauses. The most common is the fermata (or hold), which appears as a crescent shape above the staff. Fermatas may apply to notes, rests, and occasionally, to barlines.

Example 1–86

Generalpause (G.P.): A device in use since the eighteenth century to indicate a sudden long pause for all players. The letters G.P. are written over a whole-measure rest.

Example 1–87

Caesura: Popularly known as "railroad tracks," this sign, consisting of two parallel lines drawn through the top line of the staff at an angle, calls for a shorter pause than the fermata.

Example 1–88

Breath Mark: The shortest pause of all is the breath mark, used in both vocal and instrumental music to denote a very short rhythmic break.

Example 1–89

TIES AND SLURS

TIES

Ties are always written close to the noteheads, but without touching them. They should have a gently curved arch, symmetrical in shape. The direction of the curve (up or down) depends on the notational situation.

Example 1–90   Writing Ties

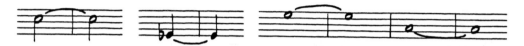

If the stems of the tied notes go in different directions, the position of the noteheads in relation to the center line is the determining factor.

Example 1–91

When a tie connects two groups of beamed notes, the tie goes in the direction *opposite* to that of the stems, regardless of the position of the noteheads.

Example 1–92

When a series of notes are tied, *each* must be connected to its neighbor.

Example 1–93

When tying intervals, the ties must be written in opposite directions:

Example 1-94

In chords with an *even* number of notes, ties are divided in opposite directions:

Example 1-95

In chords with an odd number of notes, the outer noteheads are paired off; the center notes are tied according to their position in relation to the center line.

Example 1-96

outer →
noteheads

When a chord contains the interval of a second, tie those two notes in opposition; then fill in the remaining notes of the chord accordingly.

Example 1-97

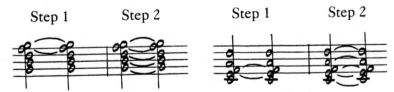

If a chord contains more than one pair of seconds, the pair farthest from the center line receives the ties drawn in opposition.

Example 1-98

SLURS

Slurs occur with great frequency and cover a variety of possibilities. They can be as short as the shortest tie or extend for an entire line. Like ties, they should trace a smooth arc and should not touch any notehead, tie, or other symbol. If the stems of the notes to be slurred all go in one direction, the slur curves in the opposite direction:

Example 1–99

If the stem direction is mixed (up and down), the slur must always go *above* the notes. Notice that the slur is drawn near the notehead of notes with stems down but nearer the end of the stem of notes with stems up.

Example 1–100

When a group of notes contains both slurs and ties, it is advisable to draw the ties first:

Example 1–101

When a tied note initiates or terminates a slurred group, the slur should be drawn to encompass both of the tied notes.

Example 1–102

If a slur would interfere with other signs below the staff, it may be written over the notes:

Example 1–103

Whole notes are slurred as if they had stems:

Example 1–104

Only one slur is needed between slurred intervals or chords; as with single notes, the slur placement is determined by stem direction.

Example 1–105

If one note of the interval or chord is a repeated or a tied note, slur the other ones:

Example 1–106

With practice, you should be able to draw nicely shaped curved lines free of wobbles and asymmetries without any mechanical aids. For a more professional look, you may wish to use a French curve (see page 144). All of the slurs and ties below were drawn with this device. Although the procedure is somewhat time-consuming, the results are invariably pleasing.

Elements of Notation

Example 1–107

DRILL

Copy the following passage on the blank staves provided below, noting the placement of rests, pauses, ties, and slurs.

DYNAMIC MARKS

Anyone using this manual has had some experience with printed music. You have, therefore, become accustomed to the shape of the traditional dynamic mark and the sight of it prompts an immediate response from you. Try, when you are writing dynamics, to imitate the traditional forms as much as possible.

Example 1–108

$pppp$ ppp pp p mp mf f ff fff $ffff$

Dynamics may be centered directly under the first note to which they apply, or they may be placed slightly to the left of that note. Both are acceptable, although sometimes one is preferable to the other (see i and j).

Example 1–109

However, all fortepiano and sforzato signs must be written directly below the note to which they apply:

Example 1–110

The wedge should be drawn with a straightedge. It is usually positioned below the staff, except when a down-stemmed note is to be played *cre-*

scendo–decrescendo throughout its duration. In that case, either method illustrated below may be used.

Example 1–111

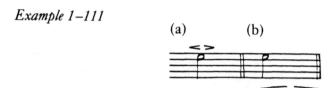

Do not draw wide wedges. When two are paired, they should mirror each other and should be horizontally aligned. Wedges should *not* follow the direction of slanted beams.

Example 1–112

If a crescendo wedge is meant to continue to another line, that line should begin with a wedge that is slightly open. The same principle holds true for a continuous decrescendo.

Example 1–113

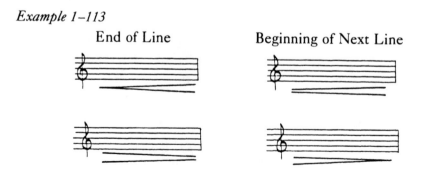

If an increase or decrease in dynamics occurs over a long stretch of music, it is advisable to use the words *crescendo* and *decrescendo* (or *diminuendo*), often abbreviated as *cresc.*, *decresc.*, and *dim.* These are *always* written below the staff, terminating with some dynamic marking.

Even more gradual changes in dynamics may be indicated by breaking the words into syllables and stretching them across the affected measures. Sometimes the words *poco a poco* (little by little) are added for further extension.

Changes in tempo, such as *ritardando* (*ritard.* or *rit.*) and *accelerando* (*accel.*) are *always* written above the staff. Here too, the words *poco a poco* may be used where tempo change extends over a long passage. Tempo changes are frequently written in larger, bolder letters than changes in dynamics. They always terminate with a specific tempo indication.

Example 1–114

REPEAT SIGNS

There are many ways to call for exact repetition, depending on the nature and extent of the passage or section to be repeated.

DOUBLE BAR REPEAT SIGNS

Use the double bar repeat sign for the exact repetition of an entire section of a work. If two such sections are contiguous, either (b) or (c) is correct.

Example 1–115

(a)   (b)   (c)

If a passage is to be repeated from the beginning of a piece, only one repeat sign is needed.

Example 1–116

The repeat sign does not necessarily function as a barline. In many cases, the sign appears *within* a measure:

Example 1–117

FIRST AND SECOND ENDINGS

The first- and second-ending forms are identical except for a terminal vertical line at the end of the second ending which is used only at the conclusion of a movement.

Example 1–118

Within a Movement   At the End of a Movement

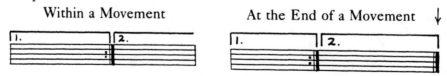

DA CAPO AND DAL SEGNO

Da Capo (D.C.) means "go back to the beginning"; it is written below the staff.

Example 1–119

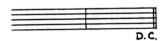

Dal Segno means "go back to the sign" (·𝄋·). The letters are written below the staff; the sign, above.

Example 1–120

D.C. al Fine means "go back to the beginning and play through to the measure marked *Fine* (end) and no further."

Example 1–121

D.S. al Fine tells you to go back to the sign and play through to the measure marked *Fine*.

Example 1–122

D.S. al Coda, a relatively rare and complicated instruction, tells you to "return to the measure with the *Segno* sign, play as far as the Coda sign (⊕), and when you reach this point, move directly to the coda." The broken line in the example below demonstrates the route being taken; it will not appear in the music.

Example 1–123

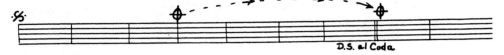

ARTICULATION MARKS

STACCATO

A small dot placed above or below a notehead indicates shortening the value of the note by one half. It is a convenient, shorthand way of indicating a separation between notes. If the notehead lies on a space, the dot is positioned in the adjacent space (above or below, depending on the stem direction). If the notehead lies on a line, place the dot in the middle of the next *full* space (above or below, depending on stem direction).

Example 1–124

When a staccato is used in conjunction with a slur, the dot is written *inside* the slur.

Example 1–125

ACCENT

This is a small wedge-shaped mark which indicates that individual notes or chords are to be played more boldly. The wedge always points to the right, is slightly wider than a notehead, and is centered over (or under) the notehead. Notice that in the example below, all the accent marks are written outside the staff.

Example 1–126

However, there are instances when accents are placed within the staff. Notice that the accent is never written on a staff line and is always at least a perfect fourth away from the notehead.

Example 1–127

When used in conjunction with a tie or slur, the accent is generally placed *outside* the curve:

Example 1–128

However, wide leaps may require that the accent be placed *under* the slur.

Example 1–129

Preferable

Not Recommended

When accents and dots are used in conjunction with slur, a more balanced appearance is achieved if the articulation marks are placed *under* the slur.

Example 1–130

Preferable

Not Recommended

However, when slurs, dynamic markings, or text are written below the staff, the accents should be placed above the notes, regardless of stem direction.

Example 1–131

TENUTO

This thin horizontal line over or under the notehead indicates that the notes involved are to be played smoothly, at full value, but not slurred. The tenuto mark is about the width of a notehead and is positioned in the same manner as the staccato dot.

Example 1–132

Like the staccato dot, the tenuto mark always goes between the note and the slur.

Example 1–133

MARCATO

This vertical wedge, which always points *away* from the notehead, signals that the note or chord is to be played somewhat louder than an accented note or chord.

Example 1–134

STACCATISSIMO

Indicating an articulation even more heavily accented than staccato, the staccatissimo sign, which is wedge-shaped, always points *at* the notehead. When written within the staff, it should lie on a staff line a fourth away from the notehead.

Example 1–135

ARTICULATION SIGNS IN COMBINATION

When articulation signs are combined, the dot is *always* closest to the notehead. If a tenuto mark is used in conjunction with signs other than the staccato dot, this mark is placed closest to the notehead.

Example 1–136

When an interval of a second is present, all signs are centered over (or under) the notehead that determines the direction of the stem.

Example 1–137

Articulation signs are written for whole notes as if they had stems.

Example 1–138

ORNAMENTATION SIGNS

TRILL

The most frequently encountered ornamentation sign is the trill, which calls for the rapid alternation of the written note with its upper neighbor.

Example 1–139

If the trilled note is tied, a trill wave is added to extend through the last tied note. This must be drawn with uniform distance between the individual waves and in a straight, horizontal line. A careful blending of up-and-down motion with a steady movement from left to right will produce the desired results.

Example 1–140

If the upper note of the trill contains an accidental, this may be indicated in one of three ways:

Example 1–141

If the trill is to begin on the upper note, this may be indicated in either of two ways:

Example 1–142

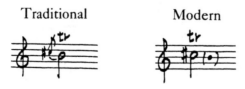

TREMOLOS

There are two kinds of tremolo: the first consists of a rapid alternation between two notes a minor third or more apart. (In string music, this is called a fingered tremolo.) Although this type of tremolo resembles a trill, it is notated quite differently, since both pitches must be shown, linked by three slashes. The total duration of a tremolo is that of only *one* of the notes.

Example 1–143

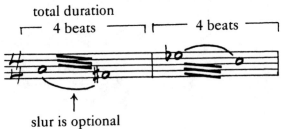

slur is optional

Example 1–144   Half-Note Tremolos

Notice, in the examples that follow, that there is a corresponding decrease in the number of slashes as the number of beams increases. In any case, the total number of slashes plus beams always equals *three*.

Example 1–145

a. Quarter-note Tremolos

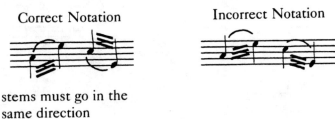

stems must go in the
same direction
regardless of noteheads

b. Eighth-note Tremolos   c. Sixteenth-note Tremolos

The second type of tremolo involves the rapid repetition of a single tone. (In string music, this is called a bowed tremolo; for woodwinds and brass, it denotes flutter-tonguing; and for percussion, it calls for a roll.) As in the tremolo described above, a total of three slashes (or slashes and beams) is required, but positioned slightly differently:

Example 1–146

With beamed groups of notes, the slashes are positioned at the same angle (left up to right), regardless of the slant of the beam.

Example 1–147

Both tremolos just described are *unmeasured tremolos:* the speed of alternation or repetition of notes is very fast but indeterminate. The *measured* tremolo, in contrast, is governed by specific, fixed note values. The notation of measured tremolos is a shorthand method of writing repeated-note figures.

Example 1–148

When a truly *unmeasured* tremolo is intended in a slow passage, it is advisable to write "trem." over the figure in order to avoid any possibility that the figure might be mistakenly played as thirty-second notes.

Example 1–149

GRACE NOTES

The stem of the grace note is always *up,* except when two parts share a staff (see page 78). Grace notes may occur singly or in groups. A single grace note is drawn like a small eighth note with an angled line through the flag. A downward-curving slur connects it to the note it modifies. This slur is independent of any other slurring in the passage.

Example 1–150

For two or three grace notes, use small beamed sixteenth notes without the slanted line, and for more than three notes, used small beamed thirty-second notes.

Example 1–151

In contemporary notation, a slash is usually drawn through any beamed group of grace notes.

Example 1–152

PART TWO

Combining
the Elements

SPACING

Good spacing of notes within a line of music ensures that the performer can perceive at a glance the different durations of those notes. This does *not* require slavish adherence to exact mathematical proportions where each measure has the same physical length:

Example 2–1

The fact is that notation that conveys the *impression* of proportion is all that is required.

Example 2–2

If you compare the next two examples (2–3 and 2–4), you will see how the effect of relative duration is achieved in Example 2–3, even though the measure lengths vary, according to their contents. Longer note values are given sufficient space to communicate the impression of their duration without wasting manuscript paper.

Example 2–3   Good Spacing

Poor spacing makes the music unduly difficult to read. The example below demonstrates another important consideration in laying out an entire
line of music: empty space, such as that at the end of the first line,
should be studiously avoided. Advance planning can guarantee that each
line is filled with complete, well-balanced measures.

Example 2–4   Poor Spacing

Occasionally, even with the best advance planning, you will not be able to
write a full measure of music at the end of a line. In such cases, the measure may be broken at one of its principal metrical points (in duple or
quadruple meter, its midpoint). Omit the barline at the end of the line to
indicate that the measure will be completed on the next line.

Example 2–5

When you are laying out a line of music, leave extra space for accidentals.
Notice, in the example below, how much more space is required.

Example 2–6

(a)

(b)

We will be dealing with additional problems of spacing in future sections, where we consider music on two or more staves. Then we must investigate the question of vertical alignment as well as horizontal spacing.

DRILL

Copy the following examples, correcting all errors in spacing.

CHANGES OF METER, CLEF, AND KEY

CHANGE OF METER

When changing meters within a piece were relatively rare, they were signaled by a double bar placed before the new meter (see Example 2–7b). Today, a new meter is simply placed to the right of the barline (See Example 2–7a).

Example 2–7

(a)   Recommended   (b)   Traditional

If a change of meter occurs at the beginning of a line, the new meter is anticipated at the end of the previous line and then repeated in the usual place. Note that the final barline is indented to allow sufficient space for the new time signature.

Example 2–8

End of Line   Beginning of Next Line

When an indication of beat values accompanies a change of meter, this information is written above the staff. The traditional method (Example 2–9a) is somewhat ambiguous because the order of values is reversed. An alternative method, used more frequently today, is recommended for its clarity (Example 2–9b).

Example 2–9

Traditional

(a)

Recommended

(b)

Even if there is no change in note values, it is advisable to indicate the equality of note values over the barline when there is a change of meter. This may be accomplished in any of the three ways shown below.

Example 2–10

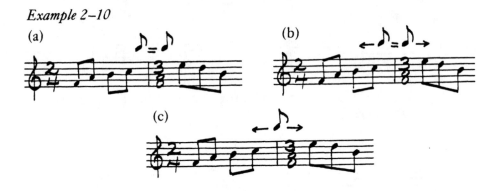

CHANGE OF CLEF

The placement of a new clef will depend largely on where the change of clef occurs. When the change occurs on the first note of a measure, the new clef, *in a smaller size,* is placed to the left of the barline:

Example 2–11

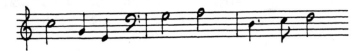

When the change occurs within a measure, the new clef is written immediately to the left of the first note affected by that change:

Example 2–12

However, if the first note affected by the change happens to fall on a weak portion of a beat preceded by a rest, the clef is inserted before the rest:

Example 2–13

Note that if a clef change occurs at the beginning of a line, a forewarning is given, as in the meter change, at the end of the previous line:

Example 2–14

End of Line   Beginning of Next Line

When a change of clef and a change of meter occur simultaneously, the clef precedes the signature.

Example 2–15

The same relationship is maintained when the simultaneous changes occur at the beginning of a line and are anticipated at the end of the preceding line:

Example 2–16

End of Line   Beginning of Next Line

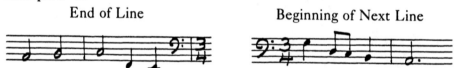

CHANGE OF KEY

A change of key is signaled by a thin double bar followed by the new key signature. Traditionally, the original key-signature accidentals were canceled before the new key signature was written, but this is now considered unnecessarily fussy.

Example 2–17

New Method   Traditional Method
(Preferred)

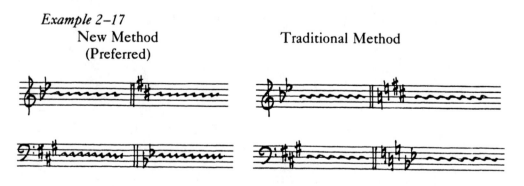

It is, however, essential to cancel the accidentals of the old key signature when the new key is C major or A minor.

Example 2–18

new key

A new key signature can never be indicated in the middle of a measure; therefore, accidentals must be used to indicate a key change until the beginning of the next complete measure.

Example 2–19   key change   new key signature is indicated
                   occurs here   at beginning of measure

When there is simultaneous change of key and meter, the following procedures should be followed within the line (Example 2–20a) and at the beginning of a new line (Example 2–20b):

Example 2–20

(a)

(b)   End of Line

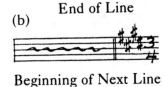

Beginning of Next Line

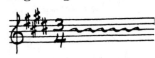

For simultaneous change of clef and key:

Example 2–21

(a)   End of Line

(b)

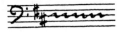

Beginning of Next Line

For simultaneous change of clef, key, and meter:

Example 2–22

(a)   (b)   End of Line

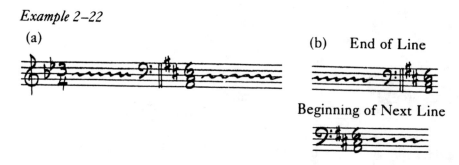

Beginning of Next Line

COURTESY ACCIDENTALS

A basic rule of notation: an accidental applies *only* to the measure in which it is written. However, there are instances when it is advisable, for the sake of clarity, to insert "courtesy" accidentals. In the example below, the second of the two C's does not, according to the basic rule, require an accidental. In performance, however, there could be some doubt as to whether the second C is meant to be a C natural. To remove all doubt, a courtesy accidental is used.

Example 2–23

Without Courtesy Accidental   With Courtesy Accidental

Even if other notes intervene, it is still often advisable to supply the courtesy accidental. Frequently you will see it in parentheses, but this is neither necessary nor recommended.

Example 2–24

Recommended   Not Recommended

Referring to the the examples below:
According to the rules of notation, the flat on the third beat of the first measure below is *not* carried over to the second beat of the next measure (a); therefore, if an E♭ is intended, the flat *must be written* (b). But if an E♮ is intended, it is advisable to write a courtesy accidental to remove all doubt (c).

Example 2–25

(a)

(b)

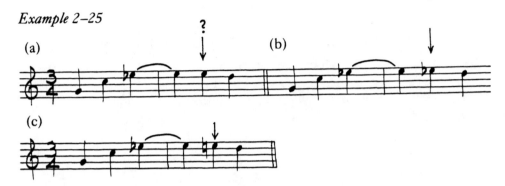

(c)

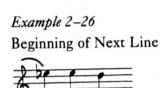

If a note with an accidental is tied to the beginning of the next line (or the next page), it is advisable to repeat the accidental at the beginning of the new line (or page).

End of Line

Example 2–26

Beginning of Next Line

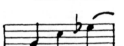

Cancellation of double flats and double sharps, formerly accomplished by a combination of a natural and a flat or sharp, is now achieved with only one accidental:

Example 2–27

New and Preferred Way   Old Way

An accidental applies only to the note at its *original pitch level*. When that note is sounded at a different octave level, another accidental is needed.

Example 2–28

Correct   Incorrect

If the octave is to be diminished or augmented, however, a clarifying accidental must be added.

Example 2–29

Notating Syncopation

The notation of rhythm should never obscure the meter. This rule is especially relevant in the notation of syncopated rhythms. All of the examples in the left-hand column below preserve the perception of the meter; those in the right-hand column do not.

Example 2–30

In examples (a), (b), and (c), beat 3 is clear.

In these notations, beat 3 is not visible.

Every beat is visible.

Only beat 1 is visible.

Beats 1 and 2 are visible.

Only beat 1 is visible.

Every beat is visible.

Only beats 1 and 4 are visible.

Beats 1 and 2 are visible.

Only beat 1 is visible.

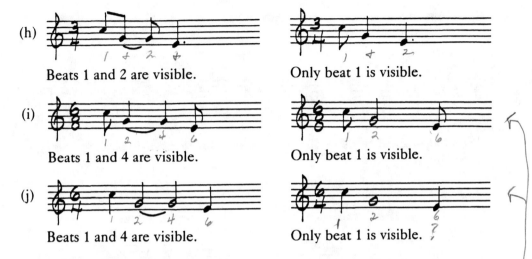

(h) Beats 1 and 2 are visible.   Only beat 1 is visible.

(i) Beats 1 and 4 are visible.   Only beat 1 is visible.

(j) Beats 1 and 4 are visible.   Only beat 1 is visible.

Inevitably, there are a number of exceptions to the rule concerning the maintenance of metrical perception. Some have been used by composers so consistently over the years that they have become commonplace. One such exception involves patterns in which a note is followed by one that is twice its duration and returns to a note of the original duration:

Example 2–31

Recommended   Not Recommended

In triple meter, the pattern may begin on the first or the second beat:

Example 2–32

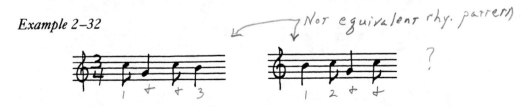

Not equivalent rhy. pattern

In 4 / 4 time, the pattern may begin on the first or third beat or both:

Example 2–33

When a pattern begins on the second beat, however, it is better to notate it conventionally for the sake of clarity:

Example 2–34

The notation of dotted notes has already been discussed in an earlier section.

Example 2–35

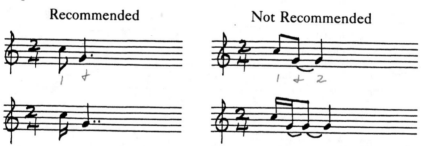

The remaining examples below illustrate several additional patterns that represent departures from the general rules governing rhythmic notation. They are all pragmatic solutions to the problem of notating extended syncopation figures in an acceptable shorthand.

Example 2–36

Recommended   Not Recommended

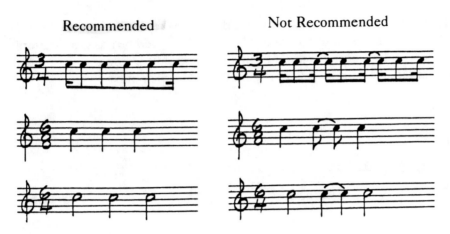

NOTATING IRREGULAR SUBDIVISIONS OF THE BEAT

Musical context often determines the placement of accessory numerals for irregular note groups such as duplets, triplets, quadruplets, etc. Generally, however, where fully beamed groups are involved, the number is centered outside the beam.

Example 2–37

If rests are combined with the beams—either at the beginning or at the end—a bracket encompassing the entire figure is added, and the number is placed in the center of the bracket. (Short brackets may be drawn freehand, but use a straightedge for longer ones.)

Example 2–38

There are two other ways to handle the beam–rest combination, both of which make brackets unnecessary: by using extended beams (see Example 2–39a) and by using extended beams with stemlets (see Example 2–39b). The latter is most effective in rhythmically complex music.

Example 2–39

(a)   (b)

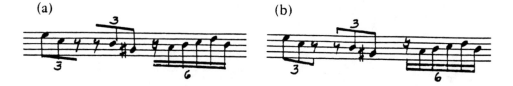

If a rest occurs somewhere in the middle of an irregular subdivision, the recommended procedure—with or without stemlets—centers the figure under the beam, although traditional notation calls for a combination of flags, beams, and brackets.

Example 2–40

Recommended   Traditional

In cases where the notes are not beamed, and all the stems go in one direction, place the number, bracketed, at the stem ends:

Example 2–41

If the stem directions are mixed, place the figure above the staff:

Example 2–42

When accessory numerals are combined with other notational elements, they will often be moved to accommodate other musical markings. In the example below, there are several situations where the overall musical requirements dictate the "misplacement" of the triplet figures. At numbers one, two, and three, the slurs above the note groups preempt the usual position of the triplet indications. At number four, the fortissimo and wedge force the triplet sign above the notes. All the other triplets are indicated in their expected places.

Example 2–43

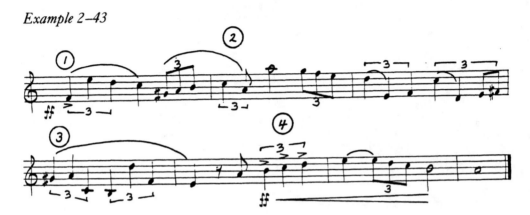

PART THREE

*Scoring
Practices*

NOTATING TWO LINES OF MUSIC ON ONE STAFF

With the exception of the discussions of intervals and chords, we have until now been concerned with the notation of a single line of notes. We will now begin to consider another aspect of notation, which will require, from time to time, some modification of the principles already established.

In orchestral scores, instrumental and choral parts, and keyboard music, two separate lines of music are often placed on a single staff. This practice not only saves space, but makes scores easier to read. However, some notational accommodations must be made.

When the two lines of music to be notated on one staff have *identical* rhythms, they may share a single stem:

Example 3–1

In cases such as this, all of the notational principles already discussed apply. However, when the parts are rhythmically independent of one another, a number of important changes must be made. Study Example 3–2 on page 79 carefully. What is immediately apparent is that the horizontal spacing of notes and rests must result in good *vertical alignment*. Let us examine the circled items:

1. Only one tempo indication is required, written above the staff.
2. If both parts share the same dynamics, it should be written only once, below the staff.
3. The lower part is always written with stems down; the upper part, with stems up. Stem lengths are about one staff space shorter than one octave.
4. Slurs for the lower part are always written with a downward curve and are placed outside the beam.
5. Slurs for the upper part are always written with an upward curve. Slurs between groups of beamed notes may be written close to the notehead.

78

Example 3–2

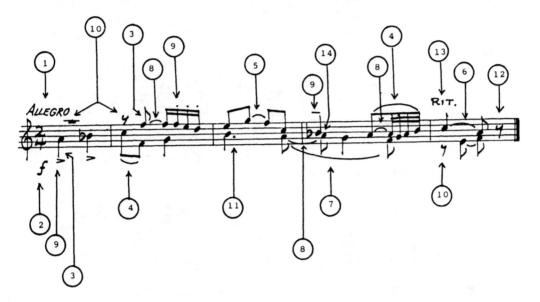

6. Slurs between two unbeamed notes may be written close to the notehead.
7. Slurs which encompass more than two notes are written outside the stems to avoid passing through any stems. The slurs terminate near the stem ends of the outer notes in the group.
8. Ties are always written next to the noteheads, even within a beamed group. They are written with an upward curve for the upper part and a downward curve for the lower part.
9. All articulation signs are written at the stem ends, never at the notehead. The staccato dot aligns with the stem itself; all other articulation marks are centered on the notehead.
10. Rests are vertically placed to avoid interference with the other part. Whole and half rests may be written outside the staff on ledger lines. Whole rests are centered in the measure, while all other rests are written in their appropriate metrical position.
11. When a dotted note in the lower part is on a staff line, the dot is written in the space below the note.
12. If a rest is common to both parts, it appears in its normal position, only *once*.
13. All changes in tempo are written above the staff.
14. When the interval of a second occurs between the two parts, the stems are aligned. Compare the placement of noteheads here with the notation of seconds written with a single stem. (See Example 1–41, page 20).

Several additional situations require clarification:

If the parts cross, the stem of the higher pitch (in this case, belonging to the lower part) is written on the left side. The noteheads must not touch each other.

Example 3–3

If the dynamics for each part are different, those for the upper part go above the staff and those for the lower part, below.

Example 3–4

Intervals and chords are written according to the principles outlined in Example 3–2.

Notice the direction of the ties for both parts:

Example 3–5

Accidentals are positioned according to the same rules that apply to single-stem chords.

Example 3–6

The notation of unisons depends upon a number of factors: are the notes black or white; are there dots in either part; are the notes flagged or beamed? Here is a variety of combinations with the appropriate notations.

Example 3–7

a. If both parts have the same rhythmic values, they may share note-heads. This is called double stemming.

b. Whole notes must be written twice.

c. Undotted black notes may share the same notehead, even if the note values are different.

d. If one black note is dotted and the other is not, the dotted note is traditionally placed to the right of the undotted note.

e. It is also considered acceptable to use double stemming even when one of the notes is dotted.

f. Separate noteheads should be used when half notes are combined with dotted half notes; in these cases, the dotted note must be on the right.

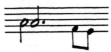

g. Double stemming is unacceptable for white notes when one of them is dotted.

h. A mixture of black and white notes automatically requires two noteheads. If there are no dotted notes, align the stems as shown here.

i. Notice that in this combination of black and white notes, the dotted note is placed to the right. In this example, double stemming would be incorrect.

j. A combination of black and white dotted notes must be written so that the stems are as close together as possible.

Preferred   Not Recommended

Review all the principles discussed in this section. Pay particular attention to the notation of tempo, dynamics, ties, slurs, articulation signs, intervals, rests, unisons, spacing, vertical alignment, crossing parts, and augmentation dots. Then copy Example 3–8 on the staves provided at the bottom of page 83.

Example 3–8

Example 3–9 contains twenty-eight errors in notation. Study and identify each one, then rewrite the passage correctly on the staves provided. When you are finished, go through the list on pages 85–6 and compare your version with the corrected one on page 86.

Example 3–9

The rhythm of the music will determine whether single stemming or separate stemming is preferable. Usually, a passage will provide occasion for using both. The unison rhythms below justify single stemming (bracketed). However, where rhythms are dissimilar, separate stemming is called for. The notation in the example below is typical of that found in orchestral scores and parts, as well as scores for keyboard, guitar, and other instruments capable of playing intervals and chords.

Example 3–10

Where unison rhythms occur for a very short time, continued separate stemming is preferable to repeated changes.

Example 3–11

The placement of accidentals depends on the instrumentation. For keyboard, or any other single instrument, the following passage is perfectly clear as written; the player will perceive any accidental as affecting both lines of notes.

Example 3–12

However, if the same passage is to be played by two instruments, accidentals must be written for each line of the music, even if that results in repetition.

Example 3–13

The notation of unisons may also be influenced by the number of players for which a passage is intended. For a single player, the following is appropriate:

Example 3–14

But for two players and the double stemming that all unisons require under those circumstances, separate stemmings are advisable for the entire passage.

Example 3–15

ANSWERS TO ERROR DETECTION ON PAGE 83

1. Tempo indication should go above the staff.
2. Dynamic marks go below the staff.
3. Stems for lower part always go down.
4. Slur should be outside the beam.
5. The dot should be in the space below the notehead.
6. The tie should connect the noteheads.

7. Articulation signs are written at the stem ends.
8. Wrong placement of noteheads in interval of a second.
9. The slur should go closer to the noteheads.
10. Wrong vertical alignment. The B♮ belongs above the D.
11. Stems are too long in this beamed group.
12. The slur should curve down.
13. The slur should curve up and be written outside the beam.
14. Tempo changes are written above the staff.
15. Stems are too short in this beamed group.
16. The ties should curve down.
17. The slur should be written lower to avoid cutting through a stem.
18. Poor spacing; the C should be placed farther to the right.
19. Wrong vertical alignment of the quarter rest. It should go above the D.
20. The rest is too low. Raise to normal position.
21. The slur should curve up and be written outside the beam.
22. Wrong alignment of noteheads in crossed parts.
23. Articulation signs should be written at the stems ends (outside the beam).
24. The tie should curve upward.
25. The dot should be written in the space below the notehead.
26. All dynamic changes are written below the staff.
27. The curve of the slur is too extreme; it does not have to begin and end close to the noteheads when there are more than two notes in a slurred group.
28. There is no need for two rests here. One suffices.

Corrected Version of Example 3–9

MUSIC ON TWO OR MORE STAVES

Before we begin dealing with notation of music on two or more staves, it is important to note that the first measure of any composition, whether for solo instrument, full orchestra, or something in between, is customarily indented. If a work is divided into several movements, the first measure of each movement is indented.

Example 3–16

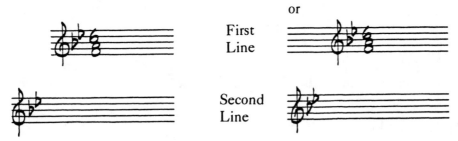

Compositions for solo keyboards (including organ without pedal), duets for single-staff instruments, and vocal duets are usually written on two staves. For non-keyboard music, the two staves are connected at the left with a *bracket*.

Example 3–17

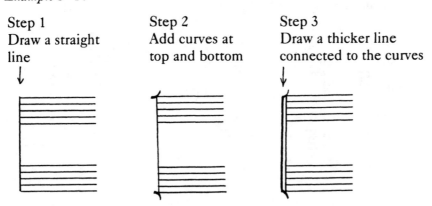

Step 1
Draw a straight line

Step 2
Add curves at top and bottom

Step 3
Draw a thicker line connected to the curves

When two or more staves are connected in this way they form a *system*. For keyboard music, the two staves are connected at the left with a *brace*.

Example 3–18

Step 1	Step 2	Step 3
Draw a straight line	Draw this curved line to the center of space between staves	Draw the same curve in reverse from the center to the bottom of the lower staff

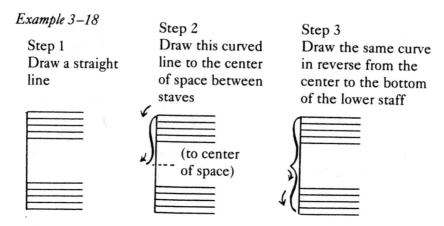

(to center of space)

DRILL

Practice adding braces to the vertical lines below.

Practice adding braces at the beginning of the two-stave systems below.

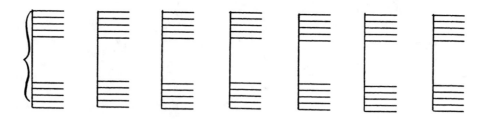

Here is a passage for two instruments:

Example 3–19

Please take note of the following points:

1. Only one tempo indication is used.
2. Dynamics are written below each part.
3. Barlines go through both parts, connecting both staves. (It is advisable to use a straightedge for these barlines.)
4. The principles of single-stem notation apply throughout, but considerations of horizontal spacing and vertical alignment are of paramount importance. Thus, the layout of each measure will depend on the rhythmic configurations of its components.
5. There should not be any unused space at the ends of lines, nor any crowding of notes within measures. This means that the total number of measures in each system must be planned in advance.
6. Every beat of every measure must be in precise metrical alignment in all parts.

Here is an example of a four-part chorale, a familiar vehicle for the study of harmony.

Example 3–20

Please note the following points:

1. There are two independent lines of music on each staff.
2. Since chorales are meant to be sung, the treble clef or upper staff is shared by the soprano and alto; the tenor and bass are found on the lower staff in the bass clef.
3. Separate stemming is employed throughout.
4. A brace, rather than a bracket, connects the two staves, since chorales are usually accompanied on keyboard instruments.

The need for careful spacing and alignment is illustrated in the excerpt from Beethoven's Septet, Op. 20 on page 91. The instrumentation, reading from top to bottom, is clarinet in B♭, bassoon, French horn, violin, viola, cello, and double bass. (A complete list of accepted abbreviations for orchestral instruments may be found on pages 129–30. Because it has the most rhythmic activity, the viola part is the basis for planning the number of measures in each system, and this part is laid in first, making allowance for the four thirty-second notes in the violin part. The remaining parts are then filled in, keeping vertical alignment in mind at all times. Notice that the system line at the left end connects all the staves, but that brackets embrace families of instruments. Similarly, instead of drawing barlines through the entire system, the barlines are also broken into instrumental family groups, making for a clearer perception of the score's instrumentation. We will discuss this at greater length when we examine score layout for vocal, chamber, and orchestral music.

DRILL

Copy Examples 3–19, 3–20, and 3–21. Examine published scores of duets, trios, etc., noting the particular manner in which problems in spacing and vertical alignment were solved.

Example 3–21

PIANO NOTATION

Probably more music has been written for the piano than for any other single instrument. Let us examine a typical piano score and identify some of the notational practices specific to this instrument.

Example 3–22

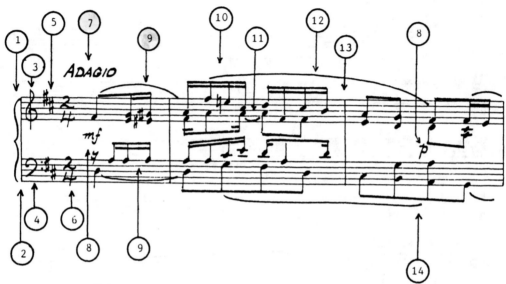

1. A brace connects both staves.
2. Next to the brace, a system line also connects both staves.
3. Ordinarily, the treble clef is used for the upper staff and music written on this staff is played with the *right* hand.
4. The lower staff usually employs the bass clef and is played with the *left* hand.
5. The key signature appears on both staves.
6. The time signature appears on both staves.
7. Tempo indications are written above the upper staff.
8. Dynamic markings are written between the staves.
9. The two accidentals in the upper staff necessitate wider spacing of the sixteenth notes in both staves.
10. Use double stemming when two lines of music on the same staff have different rhythms. (This principle was discussed earlier.)
11. Ties should be written according to rules discussed on pages 40–44.
12. Phrasing is delineated by long slurs.
13. Barlines are written through both staves.
14. When two or more notes on one staff move in the same rhythm, single stemming may be used. Within a single measure, both single and double stemming may be used.

SOME ADDITIONAL PROCEDURES

Beaming between staves is frequently necessary in piano music in order to maintain a clear division of left- and right-hand responsibilities.

Example 3–23

Slurring may occur across staves:

Example 3–24

The placement of slurs in piano notation is often irregular (or "incorrect"), since space must be allowed between staves for expression marks, dynamics, etc.

Example 3–25

Clefs may be changed to accommodate a particular registral requirement. Notice that Example 3–26 may be written in either of two ways.

Example 3–26

Arpeggiated chords are indicated in one of two ways: if the notes are to be rolled from the bottom up to the top, a continuous wavy line is drawn to the left of the chord in question:

Example 3–27

If the wavy line is broken, each chord is rolled upward from its own bottom note, but played simultaneously:

Example 3–28

If a downward direction is desired, use a downward-pointing arrow at the lower end of the wavy line:

Example 3–29

When hand assignments are unusual, use the initials "L.H." or "R.H." to indicate which hand to use.

Example 3–30

The Damper pedal: The traditional way to indicate the use of the damper pedal is the word *Ped.* An asterisk shows the point of release. A more recent, and infinitely simpler form is shown in Example 3–31b.

Example 3–31

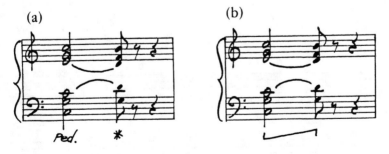

DRILL

Copy the following passage for piano, noting the various aspects of notation
particular to this instrument: brace, barlines, placement of tempo mark,
dynamics, slurs, etc.

VOCAL NOTATION AND TEXT UNDERLAY

In general, the notation of vocal music follows the principles laid down in earlier chapters, but some adjustments must be made in spacing and alignment for the words. In addition, there are several rules that govern the way the text is placed under the music.

Example 3–32

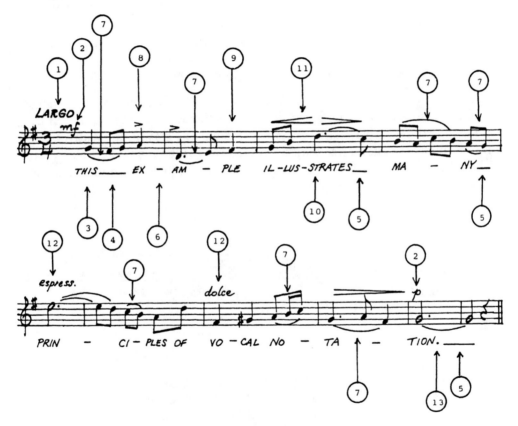

1. Tempo marks are placed above the staff, as usual.
2. Dynamic marks are placed *above* the staff, and may, on occasion, intrude somewhat into the staff.
3. Syllables within a word and one-syllable words containing up to five letters, sung on a single note, are centered directly under the note.
4. One-syllable words sung on more than one note are followed by an *extender line*, which starts at the base of the last letter and extends to the right side of the last note in the group.

5. If the last syllable of a word is sung on two or more notes, an extender line is added, as in No. 4 above.

6. Syllables of a word are separated by a hyphen; use more than one hyphen only if syllables are widely separated, and then sparingly.

7. When syllables within a word or one-syllable words are sung on two or more notes, those notes are *slurred*.

8. All articulation signs are placed *above* the staff.

9. No extender line is required for the last syllable of a word if it is sung on one note.

10. A syllable of several letters, when sung on two or more notes, may be positioned so that the second letter of the syllable is directly under the first note of the group.

11. Wedges (and all other accents) are written above the staff.

12. Expression indications are written above the staff.

13. Punctuation marks in the text precede the extender line.

Be sure that your lettering is clear and legible. Whether you use continuous upper-case letters (as in Example 3–32), or italic style, your task will be facilitated if you maintain a straight horizontal line by working with a base-line ruler.* An alternative to freehand lettering is the typewriter, but whatever means are employed in laying down the text, it is important that the words remain on one horizontal line.

Example 3–33

DRILL

Review all the principles and characteristics of vocal notation described in this section. Then copy Example 3–32 on the staves provided below.

_____
_____
_____
_____
_____

_____
_____
_____
_____
_____

*See Appendix, page 144, regarding tools used in score preparation.

Example 3–34 contains twenty errors in notation. Study and identify each one, then rewrite the passage correctly on the staves provided. When you are finished, compare your results with the correct answers on page 102.

Example 3–34

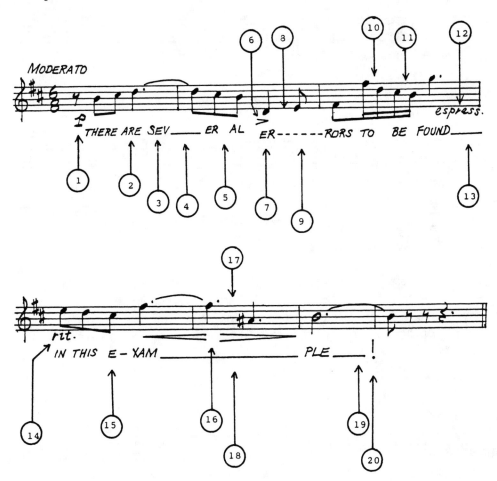

All the examples in this section, thus far, have been written according to the principles of beaming and flagging that govern *instrumental* notation. In the past, the conventions followed for vocal music were very different, and you will still find a great many old editions in which the traditional procedures were followed. The difference in approach will be instantly clear to you if you compare the two parts of Example 3–35: the traditional notation is much more difficult to read, since the irregular mixture of beams and flags interferes with one's clear perception of the meter.

Example 3–35

In music for voice and piano, three staves are used, connected by an initial system line. Thereafter, the barlines are separate. Often, some adjustment in the spacing of the accompanying line has to be made because of the text. In any case, vertical alignment must be preserved at all times.

Example 3–36

We follow many of the same guidelines in writing for two voices and piano. Only the system line connects all four staves; after that each voice and the piano is barred separately. Each voice has its own dynamic markings, but the tempo is given only once, above the score. Notice that, in the example below, the tenor part is written in the treble clef. (When the line is sung by a tenor voice it will *sound* one octave lower.) Although no further notation is necessary, a small "8" will sometimes be suspended from the clef, or two clefs used, as shown in Examples 3–38a and b.

Example 3–37

Example 3–38

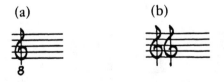

ANSWERS TO ERROR DETECTION ON PAGE
99

1. The dynamic marking should go *above* the staff.
2. Improper vertical alignment of word and notehead. The word "are" should be centered below the note C.
3. Same as in #2. The "sev" should be directly under the note D.
4. The extender line is incorrect. There should be a hyphen instead.
5. A hyphen is missing here.
6. All articulation marks should be written *above* the staff.
7. The line of text *drops* here. This should not happen.
8. A slur is missing.
9. Only a *single* hyphen should be written.
10. A slur is missing.
11. A slur is missing.
12. All expression indications are written *above* the staff.
13. No extender line is needed here, since the word is associated with only a single note.
14. All tempo indications go *above* the staff.
15. Improper syllabification. It should be "ex-."
16. Wedges go above the staff.
17. A slur, which should start from the first of the two tied notes, is missing.
18. The extender line is incorrect; it should be a hyphen. In fact, the distance here would justify two hyphens.
19. The extender line is too short; it should be prolonged as far as the right side of the last note.
20. All punctuation marks follow the word, not the extender line.

Corrected Version of Example 3–34

CHORAL NOTATION

In music for any choral combination, the system line is always preceded by a bracket. In accordance with their vocal ranges, soprano, alto, tenor, and bass (S., A., T., B.) are arranged in that order from top to bottom. Each part has separate barlines; each part has its own text underlay and dynamics. Main tempo indications appear only once, in boldface lettering, above the staff. However, tempo modifications, such as ritardando and accelerando, appear above each part.

Example 3–39

A cappella (unaccompanied) choral music often adds a piano reduction at the bottom of each system to expedite rehearsals. In printed music, this part is frequently written in small notes, but this is neither necessary nor desirable. If the part is clearly labeled, there is no real danger that it will be used for performance purposes. In the rehearsal part, slurs may be omitted, but dynamics, tempo, and time values are maintained. (See Example 3–40 on page 104.)

In simpler music, where pairs of parts move in the same rhythm most of the time, and where word placement is identical in both voices, a condensed choral score is often sufficient. Soprano and alto share the upper staff, with tenor and bass in the lower. The text is written below each staff and single stemming prevails. (See Example 3–41 on page 104.)

If all four voices share rhythmic values and word placement, a single line of text between the staves will suffice. (This is a common practice in hymnals. See Example 3–42 on page 104.)

Example 3–40

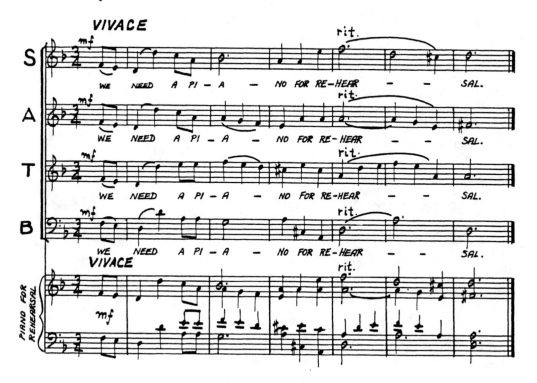

Example 3–41

Example 3–42

CHAMBER MUSIC SCORES

In score layouts for chamber groups, both small and large, the primary consideration is (1) the ordering of instruments from top to bottom and (2) the bracket and barline patterns. We have already discussed the combination of piano with voice or chorus. When the piano accompanies a solo instrument, such as the violin, the same general layout is used. However, it is becoming common practice to add a bracket for the solo instrument:

Example 3–43

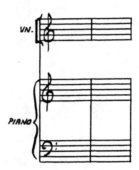

Here are the accepted formats for some frequently used combinations with piano:

Example 3–44

Two Pianos   Piano Trio (Violin, Cello, Piano)

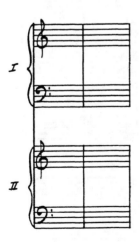
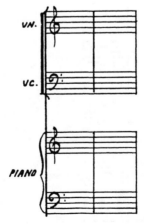

Clarinet Trio (Piano, Clarinet, Cello)

Piano Quartet (Violin,
Viola, Cello, Piano)

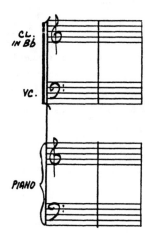

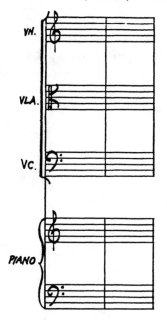

Piano Quintet
(Piano and String Quartet)

Piano and Four Winds

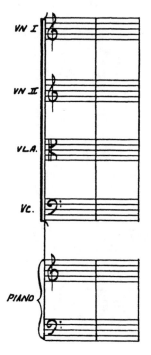

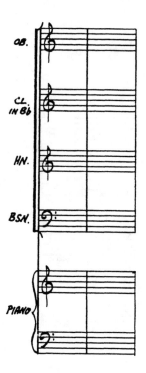

When there is a voice part combining with piano plus any instrument (or instruments), the voice part is placed directly above the piano:

Example 3–45

Voice, Piano, and Any Instrument

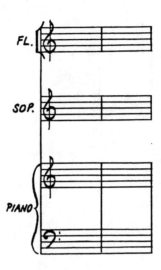

In scores for a family of instruments (strings, winds, brass), the members of that family are generally positioned according to range, from top to bottom (from high to low).

Example 3–46

String Quartet

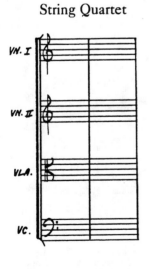

String Quintet

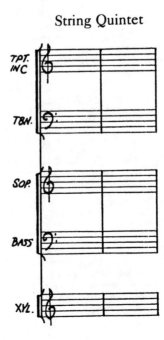

Woodwind Trio

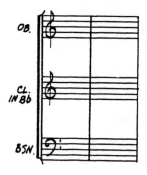

Woodwind Quartet

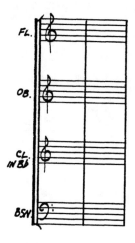

Woodwind Quintet

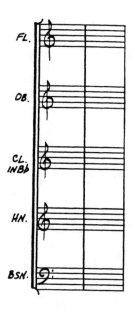

Brass Quintet

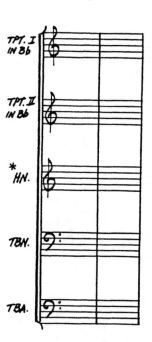

*Although the horn is clearly a brass instrument, it is often used in combination with woodwinds as part of the ensemble. In these cases, the horn is placed above the bassoon and barred and bracketed with the wind instruments. However, in a brass quintet, the horn is positioned below the trumpets. You will discover, in the section on *orchestral* scores, that the peripatetic horn often occupies yet another position within the family.

In scores involving mixtures of winds, brass, and strings, the winds are placed highest, followed by the brass, and then the strings. Each family of instruments or members thereof is separately barred and bracketed.

Example 3–47

String Quartet and One Woodwind

Mixed Families

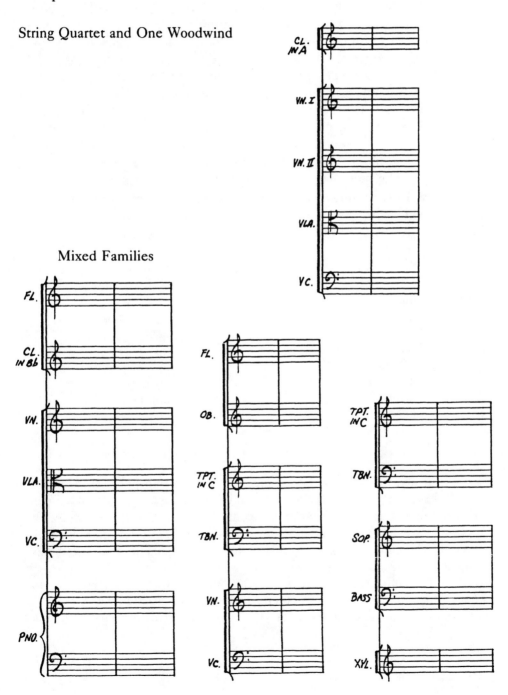

TRANSPOSING
INSTRUMENTS

Before we move on to the subject of orchestral scores, it may be helpful to discuss the question of transposing instruments, the process of transposition, and transposed scores. Not all instruments playing the *written* note middle C, for example, will actually *sound* middle C; many transposing instruments produce a different pitch altogether.

For example, the B♭ clarinet is so named because when one reads and plays the written note middle C, the resulting sound is B♭, one whole step lower. Therefore, if a piece of music is written in the key of B♭ major, the part for B♭ clarinet must be written (or transposed) up a major second, or in C major. Thus, when the B♭ clarinet plays the part (written in C major), we hear "concert" B♭ major, the desired tonality. Below you will find a summary of the most frequently used transposing instruments for quick reference. Less commonly used transposing instruments may be found in the comprehensive Instrument Scoring Guide on pages 129–30, which lists all of the instruments of the orchestra and concert band.

Instrument	*Written Pitch that Sounds "C"*	*Interval of Transposition*
Piccolo	C	down an octave
English Horn	G	up a perfect 5th
B♭ Clarinet	D	up a major 2nd
A Clarinet	E♭	up a minor 3rd
Bass Clarinet	D	up a major 9th
Contrabassoon	C	up an octave
French Horn	G	up a perfect 5th
B♭ Trumpet	D	up a major 2nd
Double Bass	C	up an octave

Traditionally, full scores are prepared with all parts transposed that require it. This accounts for the fact that several different key signatures will be in use simultaneously. For example, a composition in C major for flute, B♭ clarinet, English horn, and alto saxophone—a rather unlikely combination, but excellent for purposes of illustration—would carry four different key signatures. (See Example 3–48).

In brass music, it has been customary to eliminate key signatures in both score and parts for trumpets and horns, adding accidentals as needed in the music for these instruments. However, many scores and parts are now

Example 3–48

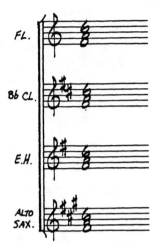

prepared with full signatures. Compare versions (a) and (b) in the following example:

Example 3–49

a. No Key Signatures for Trumpet and Horn

b. Key Signatures in All Parts

The difficulties in reading a score with transposed parts, particularly in contemporary music, has led to the creation of "C" (or concert) scores, in which all the music is written as sounded. In a C score, none of the parts are transposed except those which transpose at the octave. Here is a "C" score version of the brass trio passage in Example 3–49:

Example 3–50

Of course, when instrumental parts are extracted from a "C" score, each one must be properly transposed wherever necessary. (See page 131 for further discussion of this procedure.)

ORCHESTRAL SCORES

In this section, we will deal with notational practices and scoring as follows:

Scoring for string orchestra
Scoring for chamber orchestra
Scoring for full orchestra
Scoring for orchestra with soloist and / or chorus
The title page
Rehearsal numbers and letters
Reduced scores

STRING ORCHESTRA

In the string orchestra, the violins are usually divided into two parts, each with its own staff. These are further joined by a brace (Example 3–51a) or an additional bracket (Example 3–51b).

Example 3–51

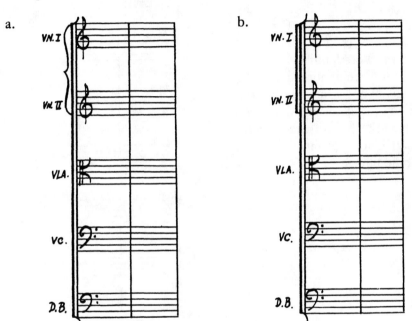

All divided instruments, such as the violins, may be labeled in either of the following ways:

Example 3–52

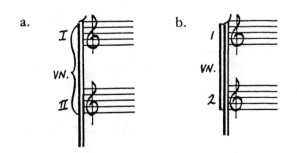

CHAMBER ORCHESTRA

Example 3–53

Example 3–53 shows the score layout for a fairly typical chamber orchestra combination. There are several characteristics to note: (1) the instrumental choirs (winds, brass, and strings) are bracketed and barred separately; (2) the French horns now take their orchestral position above the trumpets; and (3) paired wind or brass parts (such as the horns in this example) usually share one staff, provided their combined lines are not very complicated.

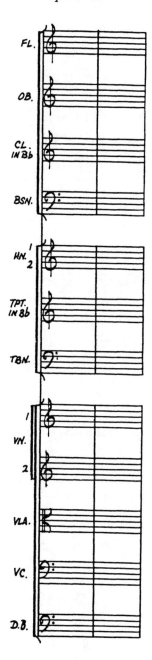

FULL ORCHESTRA

Example 3–54

A score for full orchestra usually contains paired winds, four horns, three trumpets, three trombones, tuba, percussion, and strings. Example 3–54 is a typical layout. Notice several additional characteristics of an orchestral score: (1) key and time signatures appear on every staff (note especially that in this hypothetical work in G major, there are several transposing instruments with different signatures); (2) dynamic markings appear below every staff; (3) tempo headings are placed at the top of the score and above the string section only (this applies to changes of tempo as well); (4) it is traditional, when scoring for a three-instrument group, to pair the first and second and place the third on a staff by itself (see trumpets and trombones).

Some further considerations: when auxiliary woodwinds, such as piccolo, English horn, bass clarinet, contrabassoon, etc., are added, they are bracketed and barred within the woodwind choir. They are also combined (by brace or additional bracket) with the instrument to which they are most closely related (i.e. piccolo to flute, English horn to oboe, etc.) (See Example 3–55 on page 116).

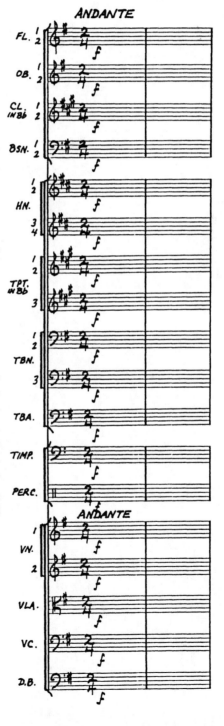

Example 3–55 Full Orchestra with Auxiliary Winds

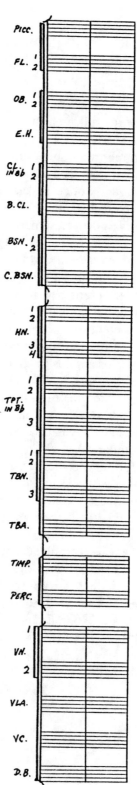

When woodwind or brass instruments are paired on a single staff, it must always be clear which of the two instruments plays which line of music. If they are playing separate lines simultaneously, then up-stems for the first chair and down-stems for the second will suffice. If, however, there is a single line of music, the notation must convey whether that line is to be played by the first chair, the second chair, or by both. For each of these possibilities, there are two acceptable solutions:

Example 3–56

a. First Chair Only   or

b. Second Chair Only   or

c. Both Play   or

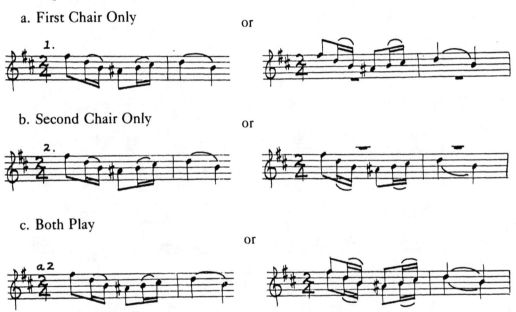

When the first and second violins are further divided, clarification is urgently required, since the passage, unless otherwise indicated, could call for each violinist to play—or attempt to play—double stops. If this is not the intention, then the word *divisi* (abbreviated *div.*) must appear above the first note in the two-part passage. When a single line of music to be played by all instruments returns, write *unisono* (abbreviated *unis.*) above the staff.

Example 3–57

In recent times, composers have looked for ways to make time signatures more prominent and less trouble. Below, you will find a variety of time-signature formats currently in use.

Example 3–58   Time Signature Layouts in Current Use

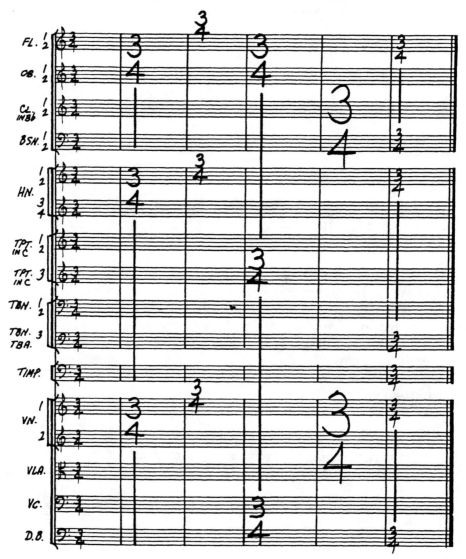

FULL ORCHESTRA WITH SOLOIST
AND / OR CHORUS

In a concerto, or an orchestral work with solo voice, the solo part is placed immediately above the strings:

Example 3–59

a. Concerto   b. Orchestra with Baritone Solo

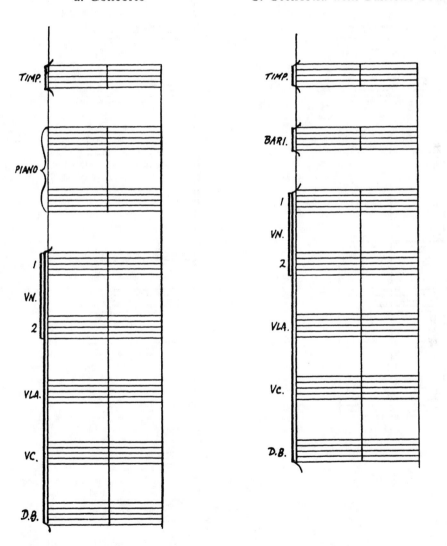

Choral parts are also written above the strings and below the percussion. If there are vocal soloists in addition, their parts are placed above the choral parts (see Example 3–60). Notice that the solo parts are neither bracketed nor braced.

Example 3–60

a. Orchestra with Chorus   b. Orchestra with Chorus and Soloists

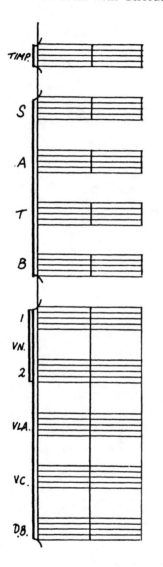

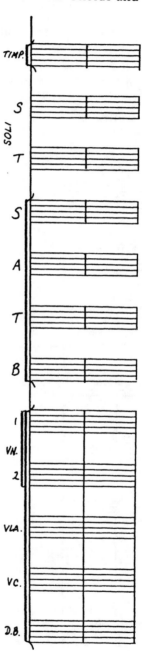

THE TITLE PAGE

There is certain information that should be included on the first or title page of a score:

Example 3–61

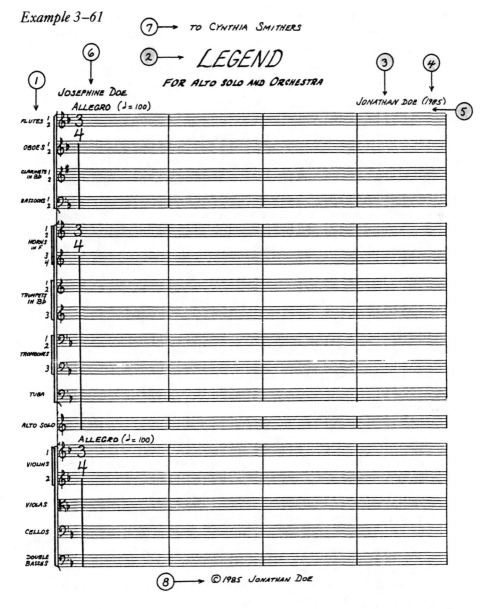

1. The complete instrumentation of the work must appear on the first page of music, regardless of how many instruments actually play in the opening measures. Here, the names of the instruments should be written out and not abbreviated.

2. The title of the work should be centered at the top of the page in bold letters.

3. The name of the composer appears at the right, just above the top staff.

4. Opus number and/or year of composition follows the name of the composer.

5. If the work is an arrangement, or orchestrated by someone other than the composer, the name of that person is placed directly below that of the composer.

6. If there is a text, acknowledgment of the author is made on the left side of the page, just above the tempo heading.

7. If there is a dedication, it is written above the title.

8. Copyright notification, either in the name of the composer or the publisher, is centered at the bottom of the page.

A great deal of contemporary music also requires explanatory notes from the composer, describing special notational devices and other highly individualized procedures that the conductor and players must understand if they are to perform the work correctly. These notes may appear on the page facing the title or on the title page itself, depending on the available space and the length of the introductory material.

REHEARSAL NUMBERS AND LETTERS

All scores (and parts, of course) must have some set of devices that will permit conductor and players to determine exactly where they are in the music at any given moment. Without such a system, it would be practically impossible to carry on a rehearsal. In a short composition, capital letters in alphabetical order placed at key points in the music are sufficient, but in longer works, it is advisable to number the measures. There are several approaches in common use today:

1. Every measure is numbered. The number may be centered above the measure or positioned just to the right of the barline.

2. The same procedure is followed as in No. 1 above, but the number is placed *below* the system (or staff) and centered. This method is favored in popular music.

3. Every five measures are numbered; the number is written above the system to the right of the barline.

4. Every ten measures are numbered, as in No. 3 above.

5. The appropriate measure number is written above the first measure of each system, just above the clef.

6. As in No. 5, the appropriate number is written above the first measure of each system, but in addition, capital letters in alphabetical order are written above the system at key musical points.
7. As in No. 6, except that measure numbers are added at key musical points in addition to the ones above the first measure of each system.

Example 3–62

The author favors No. 5, but recommends No. 6 or 7 for larger works. Whichever method you choose, an additional set of measure numbers should be added in orchestral scores above the Violin 1 part. (See Example 3–62). The numbers should be enclosed in a rectangle (or circle) for increased visibility. By placing the numbers at the beginning of each system, you keep them well out of the way of the notes themselves, a distinct advantage.

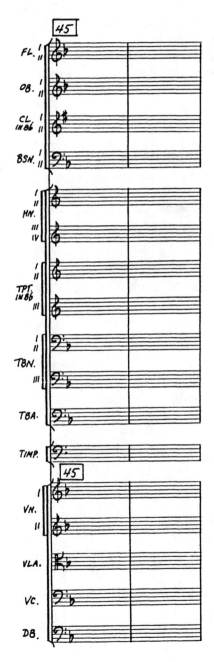

REDUCED SCORES

Once you have established the full instrumentation of a work on the title page, it will often be possible, even in a full orchestral score, to fit two systems on a page. This is accomplished by omitting all instruments that are not actually playing, and give a staff line only to those that are. The systems are separated from one another on the page by a pair of heavy diagonal slashes (see Example 3–63). This procedure not only saves a lot of space, but also serves to communicate the instrumentation at any given point to the conductor most effectively.

Example 3–63

CONCERT BAND SCORES

Example 3–64

The instrumental combinations that are found in band music are far more varied and less preordained than those of the symphony orchestra. There are wind ensembles, wind bands, concert bands, and just mixed bands. None of them have a fixed instrumental format, nor do these various names indicate relative size. As a point of departure, we may say that a wind ensemble might consist of a symphony orchestra without any strings, except, perhaps, a single double bass. Saxophones are usually added, their parts placed below the bassoons, and the percussion section might be somewhat enlarged. Example 3–64 is one possible instrumentation and layout.

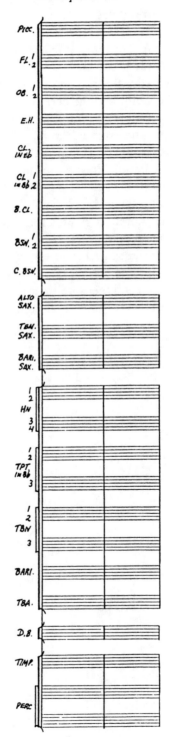

Larger bands regularly include some instruments not ordinarily found in today's symphony orchestra: cornets in B♭, baritones (same as euphonium and related to the tuba), and saxophones. Wind and brass sections are expanded beyond symphonic proportions with versions of many instruments in several different ranges. Unfortunately, instrumental disposition in band-music scores is not fully standardized, so some instruments may appear in unpredictable and unorthodox positions. In general, however, the winds are placed very much like their orchestral counterparts. Although the horns appear in their usual position at the top of the brass in wind ensembles, the cornets precede the horns in most large concert band scores. Below the horns, trumpets, trombones, baritones, and tubas, you will find the double bass (!) followed by the timpani and other percussion.

Example 3–65 (on the facing page) contains two possible layouts for concert band. Notice the position of the horns in (a) and the surprising placement of the clarinets in (b). The latter is explained by the fact that, in band music, the clarinets have become a principal melodic instrument and are therefore given a more prominent position in the score.

When planning a page of orchestral or band music, you must take into account the spatial requirements of each line of music, with priority allotted to the line containing the greater amount of rhythmic activity. Plan the space for each measure in advance and draw in all the barlines in advance. The part with the most rhythmic motion should be written in first.

Each instrument should be labeled with appropriate abbreviations (see pages 129–30) on every page of the score. In smaller chamber works, involving up to five or six instruments, this need not be done. The instruments can be named on the initial system only.

Example 3–65

a.

b.

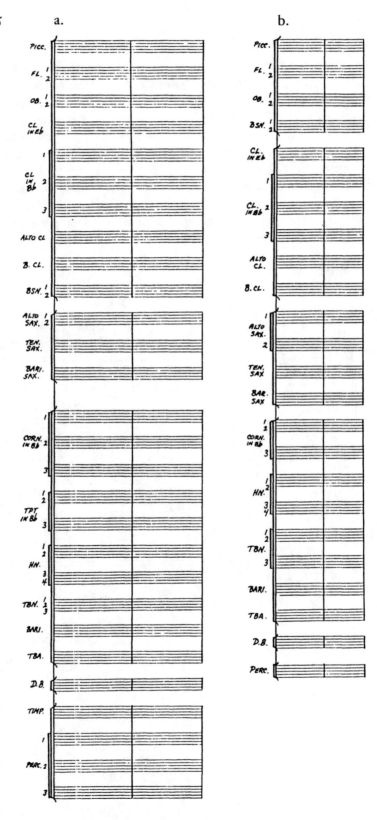

CONDENSED SCORES

The condensed score, or short score as it is sometimes called, is a simplified version of an orchestral or band score. The multistaved page on which
all instruments, suitably transposed, appear is replaced by three or four
staves, carefully labeled, on which the music is written at concert pitch.
Composers often avail themselves of this device when actually writing a
piece of music, using the shorter form as a sketch subject to change before
committing the work to full score. But this is essentially a private procedure. On a more general level, condensed scores are used primarily in
schools and in commercial music for their greater accessibility. The example that follows occupies twelve staves in full score; the only instrument
that is not readily apparent is the timpani.

Example 3–66

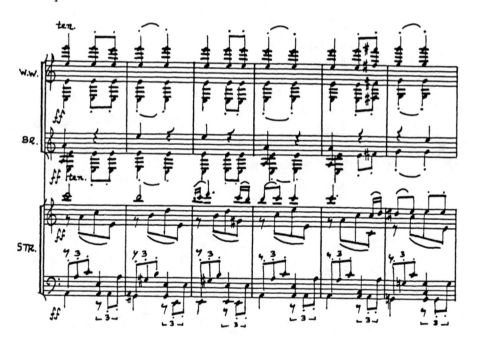

INSTRUMENT SCORING GUIDE

The chart that follows should be helpful to you in several ways:

1. It lists the instruments of the orchestra and concert band in the order in which they should appear in a full score.
2. It gives the most common abbreviations for each of the instruments, as well as some of the viable alternatives.
3. It provides the clef employed by each instrument.
4. It gives the transposing characteristics of each instrument.

Only a partial list of percussion instruments is included. For more detailed information about this very large and varied family, consult a good orchestration book such as Walter Piston's *Orchestration* or the more recent *The Study of Orchestration*, by Samuel Adler (see Bibliography, page 163, for additional titles).

Instrument	Abbreviation	Clef Used	Written Pitch Producing "C"	Interval of Transposition (Concert to Written)
Piccolo	Picc.	treble	C	down an octave
Flute	Fl.	treble	C	none
Alto Flute	Alt. Fl.	treble	F	up a perfect 4th
Bass Flute	Bs. Fl.	treble	C	up an octave
Oboe	Ob.	treble	C	none
Oboe d'Amore	Ob. d'Am.	treble	E♭	up a minor 3rd
English Horn	E.H.	treble	G	up a perfect 5th
E♭ Clarinet	E♭ Cl.	treble	A	down a minor 3rd
B♭ Clarinet	B♭ Cl.	treble	D	up a major 2nd
A Clarinet	A Cl.	treble	E♭	up a minor 3rd
Bass Clarinet	Bs. Cl.	treble	D	up a major 9th
Bass Clarinet (older scores)	Bs. Cl.	bass	D	up a major 2nd
E♭ Contrabass Clarinet	E♭ Cbs. Cl.	treble	A	up one octave and a major 6th
B♭ Contrabass Clarinet	B♭ Cbs. Cl.	treble	D	up two octaves and a major 2nd
Bassoon	Bsn. (Bn.)	bass, tenor	C	none
Contrabassoon	Cbsn.	bass, tenor	C	up an octave
Soprano Saxophone	Sop. Sax.	treble	D	up a major 2nd
Alto Saxophone	Alt. Sax.	treble	A	up a major 6th
Tenor Saxophone	Ten. Sax.	treble	D	up a major 9th
Baritone Saxophone	Bar. Sax.	treble	A	up one octave and a major 6th

Instrument	Abbreviation	Clef Used	Written Pitch Producing "C"	Interval of Transposition (Concert to Written)
Bass Saxophone	Bs. Sax.	treble	D	up two octaves and a major 2nd
French Horn	Hn.	treble, bass	G	up a perfect 5th
B♭ Piccolo Trumpet	B♭ Picc. Tpt.	treble	B♭	down a minor 7th
E♭ Trumpet	E♭ Tpt.	treble	A	down a minor 3rd
D Trumpet	D Tpt.	treble	B♭	down a major 2nd
C Trumpet	C Tpt.	treble	C	none
B♭ Trumpet	B♭ Tpt.	treble	D	up a major 2nd
Cornet	Cor.	treble	D	up a major 2nd
Fluegelhorn	Flhn.	treble	D	up a major 2nd
Bass Trumpet	Bs. Tpt.	treble	D	up a major 9th
Alto Trombone	Alt. Tbn. (Trb.)	alto	C	none
Tenor Trombone	Ten. Tbn.	bass, tenor	C	none
Bass Trombone	Bs. Tbn.	bass, tenor	C	none
Baritone Horn	Bar.	treble	D	up a major 9th
Euphonium	Euph.	bass, tenor	C	none
Tuba (all sizes)	Tba.	bass	C	none
Timpani	Timp.	bass	C	none
Vibraphone	Vibe.	treble	C	none
Xylophone	Xyl.	treble	C	down an octave
Marimba	Mar.	bass, treble	C	none
Glockenspiel	Glock.	treble	C	down two octaves
Chimes	Chm.	treble	C	none
Celesta	Cel.	bass, treble	C	down an octave
Piano	Pno.	bass, treble	C	none
Violin	Vn. (Vl., Vln.)	treble	C	none
Viola	Vla. (Va.)	alto, treble	C	none
Cello [Violoncello]	Vc. (Vlc.)	bass, tenor, treble	C	none
Double Bass [Contrabass]	D.B. (Cb.)	bass, tenor, treble	C	up an octave

EXTRACTING INSTRUMENTAL PARTS

A score must be carefully proofread before you embark on copying out parts for the players. Every pitch, accidental, slur, tie, and articulation sign—*everything*—should be meticulously checked. Transpositions will need special attention. Also, watch out for missing dynamics, tempo, and expression marks. Verify measure numbers. Whenever possible, work from a photocopy of the score when extracting parts so the original does not become smudged or dirty. This will also enable you to mark up the score with whatever symbols you need to remind yourself about tempo headings, for example, which must be included in every part.

This is the way an instrumental part should begin:

Example 3–67

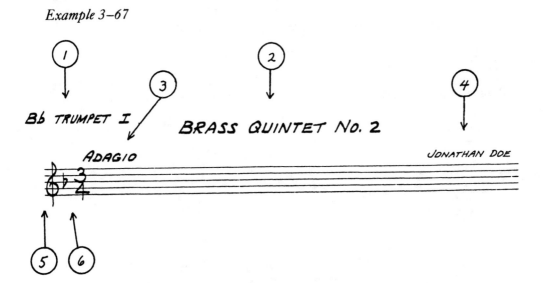

1. The name of the instrument is in the upper left-hand corner.
2. The title of the work is written above the first staff, centered.
3. The tempo heading is on the left side, just above the staff and slightly to the right of the time signature.
4. The name of the composer is above the staff on the right side.
5. The staff has *no* barline at its left end.
6. Clef, key signature, and time signature are placed as usual.

The copyright notice should appear centered at the bottom of the first page of the part.

It is not advisable to use manuscript paper on which there are more than ten lines to the page. (For more detailed information about manuscript paper, see page 144 in the Appendix.) Copy one page at a time, filling in all the necessary details. Place measure numbers at the beginning of each line above the clef and at key points in the score. When a page is finished, make sure that the measure numbers in the score and the part match. If, during the extraction process, you do come across an error in the score, go back to the original and change it immediately.

Plan the layout of each line so that the measures are well spaced and uncrowded and there is no empty staff space left over.

PAGE TURNS

Bear in mind that on the odd-numbered pages (that is, the right-hand pages) provision should be made for unhurried page turns. Look for a measure with a rest, or with relatively little activity, and plan to have your page end with it. Sometimes it may be necessary to leave a line or two blank in order to facilitate the page turn. When it is clear that the player will have very little time to make a turn, it is helpful to write *v.s. (volti subito* or *turn quickly)* underneath the last measure.

NOTATING MULTIPLE RESTS

Rests of more than one measure may be combined, as shown here:

Example 3–68

However, you must indicate any changes of meter and/or key that take place during a long rest in the following way:

Example 3–69

CUE NOTES

When an instrument has a long period of silence, its reentry should be preceded by cue notes. These very small notes present a passage played by another instrument and are clearly perceived by the player at rest as a guide to accurate reentry. Cue notes are always written with stems in one direction only—either up or down—along with full rests for the player preparing to come in. The name of the instrument playing the cue passage should be indicated in abbreviated form, and all ties, dynamics, slurs, and articulation marks are retained.

Example 3–70

If the instrument at rest is a transposing instrument, the cue notes should be transposed for that instrument. In other words, in a B♭ clarinet part, a flute passage selected as a cue must be transposed up a major second to be properly understood by the clarinet.

REPEAT SIGNS

In instrumental parts, but not in scores, several kinds of repeat signs are permissible. Repetition of a single measure may be handled as follows:

Example 3–71

If there are several repetitions of that single measure, they should be numbered:

Example 3–72

Never begin a line with a repetition sign. If a figure is to be continued on the following line, rewrite it and begin again:

Example 3–73

The repetition of a two-measure pattern is handled as follows:

Example 3–74

Do not use the two-measure repeat sign more than once. Furthermore, this procedure cannot be used if the two-measure pattern occurs in the last measure of one line and the first measure of the next:

Example 3–75

Incorrect

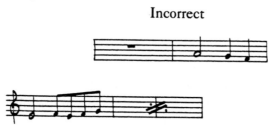

THE MEASURED TREMOLO

Rhythmic repetition of single eighth, sixteenth, and/or thirty-second notes (see page 56) may be expressed in a simplified notation, but it is essential that the fully written-out version precede the abbreviation:

Example 3–76

When written in this specific manner, measured tremolos are fully acceptable in scores as well as in individual parts.

DRILL

1. On page 136 you will find a sample page of an instrumental part. Study it carefully, noting all the specific procedures discussed in this section. Then copy out the entire page on standard-size manuscript paper.

2. Copy out one movement of the first violin part from the full score of an eighteenth- or nineteenth-century symphony, keeping in mind the principles set forth in this section. Proofread your work when you have finished.

Bb CLARINET II

SYMPHONY No. 1

JONATHAN DOE, OP. 11

V. S.

Appendix

Professional Tools And Materials

Although acceptable scores and parts can be written in pencil, the theory student, composer, or arranger who wishes to produce the kind of professional, permanent manuscript the music industry has come to expect must learn to write in ink. All of the examples in this text were prepared in ink, using the materials and techniques described on the following pages. Before discussing specific techniques, let us examine the list of basic materials you will need. As you can see, the list is not very long, nor are the items very expensive:

1. Pens
2. Ink
3. Pen cleaner
4. Rulers
5. Paper
6. Correction materials
   a. Eraser
   b. Razor blade or X-Acto blade
   c. Magic Tape
   d. Rubber cement
   e. Liquid paper
   f. Correction strips
7. Facial tissue or cloth
8. Light blue and red colored pencils
9. Crocus paper and hone
10. Typewriter and carbon paper (optional)

1. PENS

Three different pens are needed to produce a first-rate manuscript: a music writing pen; a fine-line pen; and a large lettering pen.

Music Writing Pen. You will rarely find agreement among professional music copyists concerning the best pen for writing music. At the present time, there are at least four brands of pens available, and each has its enthusiastic adherents: Osmiroid, Pelikan, Senator, and Sheaffer. They are all available with an extensive range of point sizes to suit every need.

Until a few years ago, the undisputed leader in the field was the Ester-brook fitted with a #2312 or #9212 nib; unfortunately, the company went out of business.

Osmiroid pens have a plastic squeeze reservoir for ink, while the Pelikan and Senator pens use the familiar suction-fill method, by which the ink is drawn into a transparent cylinder. Pelikan and Senator pens are twice as expensive as Osmiroid, but the investment is still quite modest. The Sheaffer No-Nonsense Calligraphic pen is a more recent arrival on the scene and is by far the cheapest of all the fountain pens used for writing music. In order to use the Sheaffer properly, a converter must be substituted for the refill cartridge normally supplied with the pen. The converter is a refill-able rubber reservoir which allows you to use the ink of your choice. There is no basis whatever for the contention that ink reservoirs will eventually erode from the carbon inks recommended for music writing. Proper maintenance and cleaning will ensure a long life for any of these pens.

It is wise to own several duplicate points (or nibs), since no two are exactly alike. You may have to experiment to find the right point for your hand. In the Osmiroid line, Italic nibs are available in Extra Fine Straight, Fine InterMedium Straight, Medium Straight, and Broad Straight, as well as Fine, Medium, and Broad Oblique. There is also a Music Point, which is available in right-hand oblique design. Pelikan and Senator points come in Italic Fine, Medium, and Broad, either Straight or Oblique, but the Oblique can be used by right-handed people only. The choice of a Straight or Oblique nib is a matter of personal taste; in either case, the same basic principles are applied. For some, the Oblique point allows for a slightly more comfortable and natural hand position; it also facilitates drawing ver-tical lines with a ruler. A Medium or Fine InterMedium works very well for most projects, but in certain circumstances, a finer point may be called for. The Extra Fine point is excellent for writing cue notes, for example. Although Sheaffer nibs come in Fine, Medium, and Broad Italic Straight, the only one of these suitable for writing music is the Fine point; the others are too broad. However, they may be used to good advantage for hand-lettering titles, tempo headings, etc.

The Italic point (straight or oblique) is eminently suited to music writ-ing because its construction allows you to draw vertical lines that are *thin* and horizontal lines that are *thick*. When exploited properly, this point will help you produce results resembling beautifully engraved music. Note the characteristic differences in line thickness and how they are achieved:

Example A–1

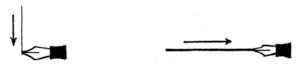

The significant difference between the straight and oblique points is the angle of contact with the paper:

Example A–2

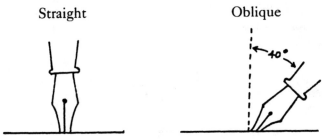

Mention should also be made of the various brands of Rapidograph pens which have found favor with some musicians but which, to my mind, have practical limitations for music writing. On balance, I would recommend one of the fountain pens described above equipped with an Italic point for all kinds of work. With one exception, all of the examples in this book were written with an Osmiroid Fine InterMedium Italic nib. The examples in the section on popular music were written with a Sheaffer Fine Italic nib (see pages 155–61).

The Fine-Line Pen. In addition to the music-writing pen with an Italic point, you will need a pen with a regular writing point (fine or medium). Both are filled with the same kind of ink, but are used for different purposes.

Italic Point	*Regular Point*
Barlines for *single* staff	Ties
Clefs	Slurs
Time signatures	Barlines connecting two or more staves
Accidentals	Articulation signs
Noteheads	Wedges
Stems	Rehearsal numbers
Ledger lines	Small words (vocal texts, *cresc.*, *dim.*, etc.)
Flags	Trill waves
Beams	Cue notes
Rests	
Braces	
Brackets	
Dynamics (*p, mf, ff*, etc.)	
Tempo headings	
Tremolo signs	
Augmentation dots	

For a minimum of pen interchange, it is recommended that you write out one full page of music using the music pen, then go over the page, filling in all of the details involving the fine-line pen.

Large Lettering Pen. For title pages and other instances where words must be prominently displayed, a large lettering pen is required. The following are reasonable possibilities:

Speedball pen with a #4 or #5 point
Rapidograph pen with a #4 or #6 point

The #2 or #3 points may be used effectively with clear plastic lettering templates available at art or drafting supply stores. If, however, you choose to letter freehand, use a beveled-edge ruler as a horizontal baseline, allowing the pen to make contact with the ruler edge. The following examples are written freehand using a Rapidograph with a #4 point:

Example A–3

ABCDEFGHIJKLMN
OPQRSTUVWXYZ
0123456789

ABCDEFGHIJKLMNOPQR
STUVWXYZ
0123456789

Of the fountain pens mentioned earlier, only the Sheaffer has a point broad enough for lettering purposes. The Sheaffer Medium and Broad Italic nibs can be used effectively, if the pen is held 45 degrees below the horizontal for right-handed lettering and 45 degrees above the horizontal for the left-hander.

Example A–4

Sheaffer Italic Medium

ABCDEFGHIJKLMNOPQRSTUVWXYZ

Sheaffer Italic Broad

ABCDEFGHIJKLMNOPQRS

Where lettering by hand proves too difficult, impressive results are possible with rub-on lettering, available in a wide variety of type style and size. This is a transfer method whereby the letters, supplied on clear plastic sheets, are rubbed onto paper one at a time. Stationery stores, art supply stores, and music reproduction shops generally stock these lettering sheets.

Ballpoint Pen—Fine Black. A ballpoint pen is recommended for restoring staff lines erased in the process of correcting an error on opaque manuscript paper. With the aid of a ruler, the original staff lines can be matched using a fine black point with care.

2. INK

Music writing inks that are a deep black, flow well, and do not clog or damage the music pen have been developed and are sold in music reproduction establishments. Designed exclusively for music copying, they can be used in music pens, fine-line pens, and large lettering pens. Heavy india inks should be avoided since they tend to clog the pens. Of the commercial inks generally available, Pelikan's Fount India is excellent and preferred by many copyists.

3. PEN CLEANER

If your pen becomes clogged and will not respond to ordinary techniques for regaining normal flow, such as wiping with a damp cloth, refilling with ink, or flushing out with warm water, then a pen cleaner is called for. This clear (sometimes milky) fluid is obtainable from most art, stationery, and music supply stores. Remove the pen point, scrub with warm, soapy water and a tooth brush, rinse, and place in the bottle of pen cleaner for a day or two. The carbon deposits on the nib will be loosened through chemical action. Rinse the point thoroughly and dry it off before screwing it back into the pen. A home brew of pen cleaner may be made by mixing equal parts of ammonia, liquid detergent, and water.

4. RULERS

The C-Thru clear plastic, beveled-edge 12″ ruler, Model B-70, is recommended for work in pencil or ink. Since you will also have need of a shorter ruler and none is available commercially of this type, buy an additional 12″ ruler and cut it in half. The resulting 6″ size can be used comfortably for drawing beams and other short, straight lines. For larger orchestral scores, a 15″ or 18″ beveled edge ruler will be required. In addition, a 12″ wooden ruler with a metal beveled edge is useful for cutting paper with a razor blade.

Though technically not a ruler, the French curve should be mentioned here. Used for drawing ties and long slurs, the French curve is a clear plastic device, shaped into a series of convoluted curves and arches of varying degrees, and offering a multitude of contours from which to choose.

Example A–5

The French Curve

Unfortunately, French curves are not furnished with beveled edges and cannot be used with ink unless the curve is elevated above the paper surface to prevent ink-smear. A few layers of masking tape, judiciously applied to the underside of the curve in several places, can remedy this situation. Throughout this text, we have stressed the faster, freehand method for drawing ties and slurs. For those feeling at all insecure about drawing freehand curves, the French curve is a ready solution.

5. PAPER

If only pencil is to be used, most classroom assignments can be accomplished on the 10-line or 12-line music paper readily available at the college bookstore. For a four-part piece, such as a string quartet, use 10-line paper and leave a blank staff between systems. For a quintet, use 12-line paper and leave a blank staff between systems. For more complicated projects, it is advisable to obtain manuscript paper tailored to your needs, with enough staves to accommodate all the instruments in your score and adequate space between systems. But it is important to remember that when you write music with ink, you must use a paper of high quality. It must be smooth, easily erasable, and capable of taking ink without feathering. Paper of this kind may be found at music reproduction stores (a list appears on page 165). Detailed, illustrated catalogues, which enable the customer to select a suitable format, are distributed free of charge upon request. Some of the standard sizes are:

> 7″ × 11″: octavo size used extensively in choral music
> 8½″ × 11″: convenient for photocopy reproduction
> 9½″ × 12½″: quarto
> 11″ × 14″

Papers designed for orchestral or band scores are available in a variety of formats.

The translucent character of onion skin (also called, variously, vellum, Deshon, or transparency) makes it suitable for reproduction by the so-called Ozalid process, employed by blueprint companies and for a long time a mainstay in the music reproduction business. An opaque, white photosensitive paper which is responsive to an ammonia process produces a durable black-print image from the original onion skin when fed through a special machine. This process has proven to be one of the most reliable methods for making multiple copies. More easily available, however, is the xerographic process, from which one can get very good results on a top-quality machine. Be warned, however: it is necessary to write the music with the staff lines on the *top side* of the paper or they will not reproduce well.

6. CORRECTION MATERIALS

Eraser. Probably the second most important tool of the copyist is the eraser. Mistakes are inevitable; the conventional hand-rub method is tedious; therefore, an electric eraser is indispensable. Though it is the single most expensive item you will have to buy, it is well worth the outlay. There are several types on the market:

> Mercury—simplest and least expensive, fits in the hand.
> Bruning, Kohinoor, Vemco, Rolex—more expensive; recommended eraser is Soft Pink (Faber-Castell #74)

Razor blade or X-Acto blade. The single-edge razor blade is used in two ways: (1) to make highly sensitive erasures where the electric eraser may be too blunt to be effective; (2) to make cutouts of manuscript paper in the event of errors of a magnitude not readily manageable with the electric eraser. Rather than erase an entire line, for example, it is far simpler and quicker to cut out a piece of fresh, blank manuscript, paste it over the original, then recopy the line. An equally effective, and less hazardous, substitute for the single-edge razor blade is the X-Acto blade, which is mounted in a handle for easy operation and control.

Magic Tape is superior to Scotch Tape in all ways. It is used for correcting errors in onion-skin manuscript which are too large for simple erasure. The faulty work is cut out with a razor, and Magic Tape is used to tape in (on the *underside*) the replacement piece of blank onion skin. Magic Tape is also used in one of the binding methods discussed later. A desk dispenser is recommended to facilitate handling.

Rubber cement. This is the only substance recommended for gluing opaque manuscript paper, since it will not curl the paper. It should be spread evenly and thinly. Its drying time is slow enough to allow for repositioning a segment. *Never* use it on onion skin.

Liquid paper. In manuscript copying (not on onion skin) smaller errors can easily be corrected by simply painting over with liquid paper. After allowing sufficient drying time, it may be drawn over with ink or, if it is slightly rough, with a ballpoint pen. If the original manuscript is to be used for performance, the liquid paper should be the same color as the paper for ease of reading. Most music supply stores and stationery stores carry a line of liquid papers from which a matching color can be found. Such matching is unnecessary if the manuscript is to be used only for reproduction.

Correction strips. For opaque manuscript paper, errors may be corrected by the application of peel-off strips. These are individual lengths of single-staff opaque manuscript paper which come in pads of twenty strips per pad. The strips are about 9″ long and can, of course, be cut to any smaller size desired. Since it is necessary that the distance between the staff lines be uniform, correction strips come in various sizes to match different staff sizes. The backing is simply peeled off and the fresh strip placed directly over the error, taking care that the staff lines are perfectly aligned.

Example A–6

7. FACIAL TISSUE OR CLOTH

A box of facial tissues should be close at hand while copying with ink to wipe off the point of the pen. Any significant halt in the writing process may result in stoppage of the ink flow. Gently wipe the tip with a piece of tissue; then try writing on scratch paper to initiate the flow again. If more coaxing is needed, moisten the tissue and repeat the process. A clean white cotton cloth may be substituted for facial tissue.

8. LIGHT BLUE AND RED PENCILS

Use a light blue "nonphoto" pencil (such as Col-erase) to make guidelines for note position, barlines, alignments, etc. Use a red pencil to draw attention to main tempo headings while copying out instrumental parts (see page 131).

9. CROCUS PAPER AND HONE

Eventually, your music pen will show signs of exhaustion: faulty action, reduced ink flow, and a tendency to be scratchy. The combined use of crocus paper, hone, and an electric eraser can restore a failing point as if by magic. Crocus paper, which is available at hardware stores, is an extremely fine-textured, abrasive paper which, when used with care, can be highly effective in reshaping the nib. With the nib mounted in the barrel of the pen and the reservoir filled with ink, very gently rub the point on the surface of the crocus paper in a circular motion, being careful never to press too firmly. Avoid any prolonged rubbing at the corners of the point. The same motion should be transposed to the hone, always applying a gentle action. The hone, a smooth, flat stone used to sharpen razors, is available at knife shops and hardware stores. As a last operation, hold the point against the spinning rubber tip of an electric eraser to fashion a smooth chisel-tip. Each phase of the process should be accompanied by frequent testing of the point on good manuscript paper or onion skin until the proper action, line size, and ink flow are achieved. Patience may be required, but the results will be well worth the effort spent. With good maintenance, a point may last for years.

10. TYPEWRITER AND CARBON PAPER

Although it is certainly possible to get along without a typewriter by printing all words by hand, it is distinctly advantageous to have one available, especially for text underlay and explanatory notes. With manuscript paper, either an ink or a carbon ribbon works well; with onion skin, however, it is necessary to reinforce the typed image by placing a sheet of carbon paper, shiny surface facing the onion skin, underneath the page. This backing will provide the added opacity necessary for satisfactory reproduction.

PROFESSIONAL TECHNIQUES
GETTING READY TO WORK

You will need a smooth, flat, hard surface, preferably a large desk with plenty of room for paper, pens, eraser, inks, and other materials. Don't work in a cramped space. The lighting should be fairly bright without too much directionality causing shadows. The chair should be comfortable and at the proper height for sitting at the desk with ease. Both arms, all the way to the elbow, should be able to rest on the surface comfortably. Always copy with your forearm resting on the surface. If possible, regulate the air temperature; in hot weather, for example, ink tends to dry too quickly.

Before filling the pen, stir the bottle of ink several times with a glass rod, wooden matchstick or some similar object. A discarded ballpoint pen refill works nicely here. It is best not to shake the bottle, as the ink will become frothy, and there may be a loss of some of the ink's ammonia. Always keep your pen well filled. When the reservoir is nearly empty, the ink will flow out too rapidly, and your pen may suddenly leave a blob of ink where you least want it.

Never press too hard with your pen. The point should move smoothly across the paper, and the ink should flow with only slight hand pressure. If this is not the case, either change to another point or treat the point with your honing materials until it works properly. To restore good flow, sometimes it is helpful merely to refill the pen with ink.

For the time being, work only on manuscript paper, but be sure to use the highest quality stock at all times. If your work is interrupted for any appreciable amount of time, put the cap of your pen firmly on the barrel and store in an upright position. If the pen is not going to be used for an extended period of time, flush the ink back in the bottle and rinse the pen thoroughly. Remove the point and scrub it in a mild soap solution with a toothbrush. Rinse thoroughly. When pen and point are dry, reassemble, but do not fill with ink until you are ready to start work again.

A good paper to use during the learning process is Alpheus Music Score Pad SP-401 or something comparable. It comes in pads of 50 sheets with 10 unmarked staves to each page, and the dimension of 8½″ × 11″ is a most practical size. Don't write on a thickness of more than one sheet of paper.

Once you have acquired the necessary materials and have thoroughly digested all of the foregoing information, you should be ready to begin copying.

BASIC TECHNIQUE

Set out a clean sheet of manuscript paper, fill your pen, equipped with Italic point, with suitable ink, and test it to make certain the ink flows well. Hold the pen with your thumb about an inch from the tip. Position the pen so that it is *parallel to the staff lines*. It should form an angle of about 45 degrees with the surface of the paper. Don't grasp the pen too tightly; there should be no discomfort or tension in your hand.

The Downstroke. Following the instructions given in Part One on page 18, draw a series of barlines, evenly spaced, across the page. As you do so, concentrate on keeping the pen parallel to the staff lines while maintaining the 45-degree angle. Don't use a ruler at this time. Continue drawing the barlines until you feel confident with the downstroke, pen position, and angle.

Guidelines for the various facets of notation are given below. Spend sufficient time with each before moving on to the next. Don't hurry, and watch that you don't tense up.

Noteheads. With no change of pen position, draw a random series of note-heads, striving for uniformity and consistency.

Stems. Add the downstroke to the noteheads and draw a random series of quarter notes and half notes. Check your pen position and angle from time to time.

Ledger lines. These may be written either with the pen in normal position or shifted at right angles to the staff lines. The latter method is more time consuming because of the need to shift pen position. Most copyists prefer keeping the pen in normal position (see page 15). Draw a series of ledger lines above and below the staff, either freehand or using the 6″ beveled-edge ruler, while holding the pen in normal position.

Clefs. Draw a series of clefs—all four kinds—across the page, keeping the pen in normal position.

Accidentals. Write groups of sharps, flats, and naturals with pen in normal position. This will automatically result in perfect accidentals with thin vertical lines and thick horizontals.

Flags. Keeping normal pen position, draw eighth notes across the page, then sixteenth notes, and finally thirty-second notes.

Rests. All rests can be written with the pen in normal position, but the shape of the quarter rest is more perfectly achieved by raising the pen 45

degrees above the horizontal for right-handed people and 45 degrees below
the horizontal for the left-handed. Compare the quarter rest that results
when the pen is held in normal position and when it is raised 45 degrees.

Example A–7

a. Pen in Normal Position
(Parallel to Staff Lines)

b. Pen Held 45 Degrees above
Horizontal

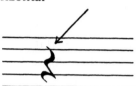

Write a line of quarter rests with the pen raised (or lowered) 45 degrees as
in Example A–7b.

Beams. Always use a ruler for drawing beams. Use the 6″ beveled-edge
ruler. Grasp it firmly and lift the upper edge about 20–30 degrees above
the paper surface. Draw the beams along the bottom edge of the ruler,
which is flush with the paper. Regardless of stem direction, always work
upwards as you draw beams. To save time, always apply the following procedure:

Example A–8

a. Draw Noteheads   b. Draw Outer Stems   c. Draw Inner Stems

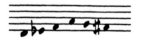      

d. Draw Beams from Bottom *Up*   e. Finished Product

   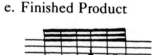

Copy this group of notes, following the routine described above.

N.B.: Be sure that the ink in the noteheads and stems is dry before you start drawing the beams. One way of ensuring this is to write out an entire line of notes before drawing any beams.

Dynamics. Write all dynamic signs, other than wedges and words, with the music pen in normal position.

Braces. This elegant shape is somewhat difficult to master. Position the pen 45 degrees below the horizontal for the top half, and 45 degrees above the horizontal for the bottom half (just the opposite for left-handers). Practice joining two staves together with a brace outside the barline several times.

Brackets. Use a ruler and the music pen. The curved lines are drawn in normal pen position. Join 2, 3, and 4 staves together with brackets outside the barline.

Augmentation Dots. Write these with the music pen. Although the staccato dot is exactly the same, it is done with the fine-line pen, which is used for all articulation signs.

Main tempo headings, changes of tempo, tremolo slashes, fermatas, and trill signs are all done with the music pen. Diligent practice of each element listed above will lead to a fast and attractive technique.

DRILL

Copy the example on the next page, in which all of the functions of the Italic nib are utilized. It takes no special instruction to handle the fine-line pen; just make sure the ink flow is smooth and the point is not scratchy. Hold the pen comfortably and leave your arms free to move. Both elbows should rest easily on the desk to allow for a smooth motion across the paper, particularly for long slurs. Once you have done a page of music with the music pen, finish with your fine-line, adding all ties, slurs, articulation signs, wedges, measure numbers, small words, trills, and cue notes.

When you feel comfortable with both the music pen and the fine-line pen, practice by copying examples from this text. A suggested sequence might be:

Exercise	Page	Exercise	Page	Exercise	Page
1-1	3	1-114	47	3-21	91
1-3	4	2-43	75	3-23	93
Drill	14	3-8	82	3-26	100
Drill	17	3-10	84	3-37	101
1-64	29	3-19	89	3-40	104
Drill	31	3-20	89		

REPRODUCTION AND BINDING

Once the score has been written—whether on opaque manuscript paper or onion skin—a practical means for reproducing and binding the finished product must be found.

Onion-skin manuscripts can be handled only by special machines that are found in music reproduction shops. You will be charged so much per page, depending on the dimension of the page. Price lists can be obtained free of charge by writing to the music reproduction store you intend to use (see listing on page 165). Onion-skin manuscripts may be sent to any of these firms by mail (Special Fourth Class is acceptable) or UPS, and returned in the same way.

For opaque manuscript scores, xerography is very inexpensive if the scores are prepared on 8½″ × 11″ paper. The major disadvantage of this method of reproduction is that most photocopy machines use very thin, 20 pound paper. (Paper used in onion-skin reproduction is anywhere from 60 pound to 80 pound, for example). If only 20 pound paper is available, print on one side only and bind with the accordion method described below. If a sturdier paper is available, you can photocopy on both sides and fashion a workable score by using a three-hole-punch loose-leaf binder. For a long score, however, a plastic comb binding, offered by many copy shops, is infinitely preferable.

The four ways of binding a score are:

1. accordion fold;
2. book style, with saddle stitch;
3. plastic comb binding;
4. thermal binding.

Accordion fold is practical for scores of no more than twenty pages. The music is reproduced on one side of a continuous sheet of paper, which is then folded in the manner shown below. This system is widely used for parts, for it obviates the need for elaborate page-turning maneuvers. (See Example A–9 on page 154.)

Book style with saddle stitch is used only with onion-skin manuscript. The finished product resembles a magazine with the center fold secured with staples. The saddle is the middle of the book and the stitch refers to

Example A–9

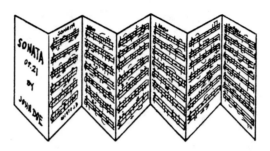

the method of fastening the pages together, in this case by stapling. This style is practical for scores up to thirty-five pages in length. It is also eminently suitable for instrumental parts.

Plastic comb binding. For scores that are longer than thirty-five pages, this is the most secure kind of binding. It is somewhat more costly than the alternatives listed above, both for the comb and for the cover stock required.

Thermal binding. In this process, pages are reproduced back-to-back on separate pages and bound like an inexpensive paperback. The left edge of each page is coated with a layer of gluing material and the score is pressed together under heat. The results are by and large excellent, but, after some use, pages tend to fall out.

Whatever binding system is chosen, the final product—conductor's score or instrumental parts—should be able to lie open on a music stand.

POPULAR-MUSIC NOTATION

Throughout this book, we have been speaking about the traditional approaches to traditional art-music. Wherever possible, the emphasis has been on emulating engraved music, with minor exceptions. The development of an efficient, freehand technique with a minimum of technical aids has been established as a desirable goal. Such a technique will serve one well, especially where music for the concert hall and/or publication is being prepared.

For popular music, however, certain notational procedures and writing methods have become common practice. In the performance capitals of the world, a great deal of music is written out which is to be read and performed *only once:* at a recording session. Whether for TV, LP, film, or other media, the scores prepared for these sessions depart from traditional notation in a number of ways, which have become standardized in the popular-music field:

1. Many musical symbols are exaggerated in size and shape for more immediate recognition by performers.
2. The music pen (with Italic nib) is used for many of the functions normally assigned to the fine-line pen: wedges, ties, slurs, all articulation signs, and all words.
3. The 30°–60° right triangle mentioned at the beginning of this book is very widely used in popular music notation. In order to use this

Example A–10

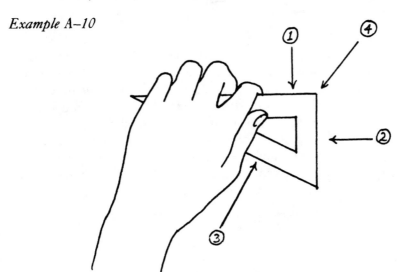

triangle, you must lift it with your hand so that its top edge ① is elevated above the paper about ¼". That top edge is used for drawing all ledger lines, beams, and wedges. The vertical edge ② is used for all straight vertical lines, stems, barlines, portions of accidentals, etc. The hypotenuse ③ is flush with the paper, but the corner of the triangle ④ is raised.

Alternatively, you can avoid the need for holding the triangle above the paper by gluing two smooth-surfaced elevators *underneath* two corners of the triangle. The elevators may be any convenient small object, such as a button, washer, or the brass heads of paper fasteners. The left-hand corner of the triangle ① makes contact with the paper. The right-hand edge, where the elevators ② are, should be raised ⅛th" to ³⁄₁₆th" above the surface.

Example A–11

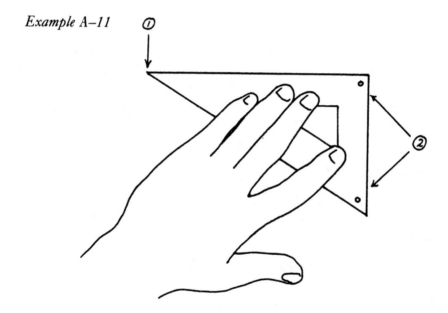

The triangle is held constantly during the copying process, moving along with your work as you proceed from left to right across the page. From time to time it is necessary to wipe off the edges with facial tissue (or cloth) to remove the accumulation of ink which inevitably forms as you write. Care must always be taken not to smear what you have just written as you move the triangle along the paper. The pace of your work will be very slow at first, but a reasonably swift technique can be acquired with practice. The ever-present role of the triangle, held constantly in the left hand,* is

---

*The left-handed person will reverse all these instructions. The triangle will be held with the right hand and the vertical edge will be on the left side.

burdensome at first, and the lack of freedom of hand movement is frustrating, but an adjustment of these factors will eventually develop. The rewards of consistently straight vertical lines can sufficiently compensate for the sense of inconvenience. This method can also be of great help to those who are, despite much practice, unable to produce a satisfactory freehand vertical line.

The example below illustrates several notational procedures characteristic of popular music:

Example A–12

1. Notice that the vertical line of the treble clef is drawn with the aid of the triangle (as are C clefs).
2. The time signature is enlarged.
3. A curved line is drawn just after the time signature. When there is no time signature, the curved line is placed after the key signature.
4. Ledger lines are drawn with the triangle, with the music pen in normal position.

Popular-music notation differs from its traditional counterpart in several other respects:

Spacing. In most popular-music manuscripts, four measures per line is the norm, except where rhythmic content necessitates *fewer* measures.

Example A–13

Articulation signs. *All* articulation signs are drawn *above* the staff, regardless of stemming.

Example A–14

Popular

Traditional

Repeat signs. To attract attention to all double-bar repeat signs, add a curve above and below the staff.

Example A–15

For back-to-back repeats, use either of the following variants:

Example A–16

When first and second endings are required, place a thin double bar at the beginning of the first ending for emphasis.

Example A–17

Place a number 2 over a repeated two-measure passage:

Example A–18

In popular-music notation, repeated figures within a measure are indicated by a slash, as follows:

Example A–19

Irregular subdivisions of the beat. Accessory numbers are placed *above* the notes, regardless of stem direction. They are *always* bracketed.

Example A–20

Trills: Write a wavy line above *all* trills, whether tied to the next note or not.

Example A–21

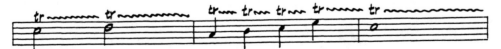

If an accidental is required, indicate as shown below:

Example A–22

Tremolos: For all tremolos involving half notes, use the following form:

Example A–23

Change of meter. Meter changes can occur quite frequently in popular music. To catch the performer's eye, use a double bar before each meter change.

Example A–24

Words. All words, including song texts, are written in capital letters. All tempo and expression indications should be boxed.

Example A–25

DRILL

The short piece below incorporates much of the material discussed in this section. Copy it, using the writing techniques and notational methods that are particular to popular music.

Bibliography

Ades, Hawley, *Choral Arranging*. Shawnee Press, 1966.
  Contains a short chapter on scoring problems, with some useful suggestions regarding choral notation.

Adler, Samuel. *The Study of Orchestration*. W. W. Norton, 1982.
  An exhaustive and important treatise which includes the latest developments in orchestral and instrumental treatment. Highly recommended as a supplement to this text.

Blatter, Alfred. *Instrumentation / Orchestration*. Longman, 1980.
  An extremely thorough examination of all the instruments of the orchestra, as well as instruments not normally associated with the orchestra, such as the recorder, guitar, and the complete range of saxophones. The first chapter gives hints on score preparation. Explores contemporary techniques and symbols used by modern composers.

Boehm, Laszlo. *Modern Music Notation*. Schirmer Books, 1956.
  A handy, compact reference book in basic musical notation. Contains no working instructions in score preparation.

Bousted, Alan. *Writing Down Music*. Oxford University Press, 1970.
  Useful in terms of some contemporary notational practice.

Brindle, Reginald Smith. *Contemporary Percussion*. Oxford University Press, 1970.
  A particularly useful book regarding percussion notation, especially the symbol notation now so widely adopted. An excellent reference book on percussion.

Cage, John. *Notations*. Free Press of Glencoe, 1969.
  Instructive and entertaining by virtue of the hundreds of examples of pages from original manuscripts by contemporary composers, ranging from the conservative to the most flagrantly avant-garde.

Donato, Anthony. *Preparing Music Manuscript*. Prentice-Hall, 1963.
  This highly informative text has recently been reissued by Amsco Music Publishing Co. Excellent instruction in notation. Materials and writing techniques are somewhat obsolete.

Kennan, Kent. *The Technique of Orchestration*. Prentice-Hall, 1983.
  In its third edition, this well-known text has been considerably updated to include contemporary techniques. Some guidelines for preparing manuscript are given.

Piston, Walter. *Orchestration*. W. W. Norton, 1955.
   For decades this book has been a recognized leader in texts on orchestration. Materials and techniques of score preparation are not included.

Read, Gardner. *Modern Rhythmic Notation*. University of Indiana Press, 1978.
   An in-depth examination of contemporary rhythmic notation.

————. *Music Notation*. Crescendo Books, 1969.
   An extremely thorough exploration of musical notation, both traditional and modern. Despite minimal treatment of writing techniques and materials, a recommended reference book.

Risatti, Howard. *New Music Vocabulary*. University of Illinois Press, 1975.
   A guide to notational signs in contemporary music. Well organized and highly instructive, it provides valuable information about contemporary notational practices.

Roemer, Clinton. *The Art of Music Copying*. second ed. Roerick Music, 1984.
   An instructional manual which specializes in the methods used in the commercial field. Excellent in terms of the technical development of the copyist, but its focus away from concert music makes it more suitable for those interested in popular music. In this respect it is unexcelled.

Rosecrans, Glen. *A Music Notation Primer*. Pen Pusher Publications, 1976.
   Limited in scope, this small treatise is similar in concept to the Roemer book listed above, with emphasis on commercial music and popular music notation. Materials and techniques are dealt with in detail.

Rosenthal, Carl A. *A Practical Guide to Music Notation*. MCA, 1967.
   Informative in terms of traditional notation. The text does not concern itself with score preparation techniques.

Ross, Ted. *The Art of Music Engraving and Processing*. Hansen Books, 1970.
   Very detailed in terms of notation. Contains interesting insights into the various methods or preparing music for publication, including autograph work.

Stone, Kurt. *Music Notation in the Twentieth Century*. W. W. Norton, 1980.
   The most important book on notation in recent years, written by a foremost authority on the subject. Invaluable not only for modern notation but for traditional notation as well. Contains no information on score preparation.

Warfield, Gerald. *How to Write Music Manuscript (In Pencil)*. McKay, 1977.
   A useful primer by an American composer and musicologist, it deals only in writing in pencil. Not exhaustive.

Wilson, Harry Robert. *Choral Arranging*. Robbins, 1949 (out of print).
   An informative text in choral arranging by a composer of semipopular music. Contains a chapter on choral scoring, layout, and notation.

Companies Specializing in Music Manuscript Reproduction and Score Materials

California
Alpheus-Cameo Music
5619 Auckland Ave.
North Hollywood, CA 91601

Judy Green Music
1643 Cahuenga Blvd.
Hollywood, CA 90028

Valle Music Reproduction
12441 Riverside Drive
North Hollywood, CA 91607

Illinois
Huey Company
19 South Wabash Ave.
Chicago, IL 60603

New York
ABC Music Reproduction Service
1633 Broadway
New York, NY 10019

Associated Music Copy Service
333 West 52nd St.
New York, NY 10019

Circle Blueprint Company
225 West 57th St.
New York, NY 10019

Independent Music Publishers
215 E. 42nd St.
New York, NY 10017

INDEX